The Stoic Path to Wealth

·THE·
Stoic Path
·TO·
Wealth

Ancient Wisdom for Enduring Prosperity

Darius Foroux

PORTFOLIO · PENGUIN

Portfolio / Penguin
An imprint of Penguin Random House LLC
penguinrandomhouse.com

Most Portfolio books are available at a discount when purchased in quantity
for sales promotions or corporate use. Special editions, which include personalized
covers, excerpts, and corporate imprints, can be created when purchased
in large quantities. For more information, please call (212) 572-2232
or e-mail specialmarkets@penguinrandomhouse.com. Your local
bookstore can also assist with discounted bulk purchases using
the Penguin Random House corporate Business-to-Business
program. For assistance in locating a participating retailer,
e-mail B2B@penguinrandomhouse.com.

Library of Congress Cataloging-in-Publication Data
Names: Foroux, Darius, author.
Title: The stoic path to wealth : ancient wisdom for
enduring prosperity / Darius Foroux.
Description: [New York, NY] : Portfolio/Penguin, [2024] |
Includes bibliographical references and index.
Identifiers: LCCN 2023030801 (print) | LCCN 2023030802 (ebook) |
ISBN 9780593544150 (hardcover) | ISBN 9780593852255 (international edition) |
ISBN 9780593544167 (ebook)
Subjects: LCSH: Finance, Personal. | Investments. | Wealth.
Classification: LCC HG179 .F579 2024 (print) | LCC HG179 (ebook) |
DDC 332.024/01—dc23/eng/20231204
LC record available at https://lccn.loc.gov/2023030801
LC ebook record available at https://lccn.loc.gov/2023030802

Printed in the United States of America
1st Printing

Book design by Jennifer Daddio / Bookmark Design & Media Inc.

Contents

Principle Three

Compound Your Money

Stoic Investing Techniques

Why Stoicism Helps to Build Wealth

· 1 ·

My Pursuit of
Enduring Prosperity

was born in Tehran at the height of the war with Iraq, in
1987. One year later, my mother left the country for the Netherlands, where she already had family members who had
made the same move several months earlier. My father wasn't
allowed to leave the country during a war, so my mother had to
make the trip alone. When she arrived at the Dutch immigra-
tion services, she had no money and just one suitcase; that was
all. My father arrived in 1990 without any possessions. He had
needed to travel by land, which took him nearly two months. It
sounds dramatic, but it's the story of millions of people around
the world. If you're living in the United States, the land of immigrants, your parents, grandparents, or great-grandparents
probably came to the country under similar circumstances.

Everyone who leaves their birth country out of necessity
needs to start from nothing. My parents had to get educated
again, learn a new language, adapt to a different culture, build
a social life, and build a better future for themselves, my
brother, and me. For as long as I can remember, our family
lived paycheck to paycheck; we were up to our necks in debt.
In our house, everything revolved around money, or rather
the *lack* of it.

My parents did their best to raise us comfortably, but they always argued about the price of everything, from groceries to clothes. Despite our limited means, my brother and I never went to bed hungry and even had a Nintendo gaming console. But somehow, I felt guilty. Like I was the cause of their financial problems. Even though I didn't know the exact details of the financial struggles of my parents, I could sense the constant tension in the house. I was afraid of losing everything we had. A recurring thought of mine was *If they didn't have me, they wouldn't have to spend all this money and they would not argue.* I realize now these were the thoughts of an overly responsible child. But my childhood did instill a sense of urgency in me. I was determined to become rich so we wouldn't have to live that way anymore.

That's what led me to pursue business and finance in college. I remember how my classmates struggled mightily choosing the right major. To me, it wasn't even a question. My only goal was to make a lot of money. And I believed that having a business degree was the highest-probability path to my goal.

In 2007, when I was still in college, I got a job at ING, a Dutch multinational bank. ING was on an international tear at the time, with offices across the globe. This was before the global financial crisis, and the industry was a lot less regulated than it is now. In the evenings I worked at ING, initially in the personal banking division, where I helped clients with mundane tasks like requesting credit cards or applying for personal loans. After three months of selling a lot of credit cards to clients, I was offered a position as mutual funds adviser in the investing division. It was a dream come true. In my teens, I had loved the world of finance that was glorified in movies like *Wall Street* and *Boiler Room.* When I received that opportunity, I imagined myself selling stocks on the phone just like Charlie Sheen's character, Bud Fox, in *Wall Street.* I didn't sell stocks of individual companies like Bud did, but I sold mutual funds, baskets of stocks, which was close enough for me. I *felt* like a stockbroker.

It was astonishingly easy to become an adviser in the Dutch financial services industry at the time. I participated in a three-week training program, and I was good to go. My assignment was simple: call existing clients who already invested in other financial products and persuade them to invest money in the latest mutual funds that the bank had introduced. The pitch was glorious, and calling clients was a great experience. This was a time when people actually loved talking to someone at their bank, when people still trusted bankers.

Looking back, however, I can't help but think, *How on earth could a twenty-year-old kid with a three-week training program advise clients about what they should invest in?* It was all about profit. The bank would consistently release new mutual funds with specific themes like sustainable energy, emerging markets, technology, you name it. A mutual fund is a basket of stocks that are picked by a fund manager. When you invest in these funds, you piggy-back on the potential success of the fund manager. The goal was to sign up as many investors as we could, because the bank earned a fee on the money clients would invest. And signing up clients was easy, because who can resist the promise of earning money without working for it? Just invest money in a fund and wait till you get rich.

After my first few deals, I thought I was an investing genius. I talked about my work with everyone: my family, friends, fellow students, professors. I even bought shares of ING with the money I made at the bank. Immediately after I bought the stock, I was rubbing my hands together, waiting to get rich myself. I bought the stock for around $27. But one year later, ING Direct was trading around $3. I had started investing at the height of the housing market bubble that caused the financial crisis of 2008–9. I felt sick to my stomach when I lost that much money. It was a feeling that haunted me for years.

While I didn't sell at the bottom, I held on to the stock until 2011, when I finally couldn't take the emotional roller coaster anymore and sold it at around $11 a share. I had lost 60 percent of my money in four years. Meanwhile, the broader market had already recovered its losses and was even higher than before the financial crisis. While I invested only around $2,000, losing more than half of what you have hurts no matter what the dollar amount is. As if the pain of growing up with financial struggles weren't enough, I got burned in the stock market too. Investing was too hard. Like everyone who loses money in the stock market, I thought it was for rich people or Wall Street bankers with three-piece suits. Even though I had a master's degree in business administration and specialized in finance by that time, I had no confidence in building wealth through the stock market. I had given up the day I sold my stock.

The truth is we can't afford to *not* invest. Everyday life is getting more expensive. The prices of groceries, gas, insurance, energy, and almost everything else are going up. Many people can't afford to buy a house. What's worse, not all wages are keeping up with inflation. In reality, your wealth is either stagnating or decreasing every year . . . unless you own assets. The graph on the next page shows what inflation does to your cash over time. Between 1980 and 2022, inflation averaged 3.06 percent a year in the U.S. (that includes the high inflation of 2021 and 2022).

In comparison, the market (when I talk about "the market," I am always referring to the S&P 500 index, which contains the five hundred largest publicly traded U.S. companies) achieved an 11.44 percent average annual return since 1980. Returns since the 1928 inception of the S&P 500 have been roughly 10

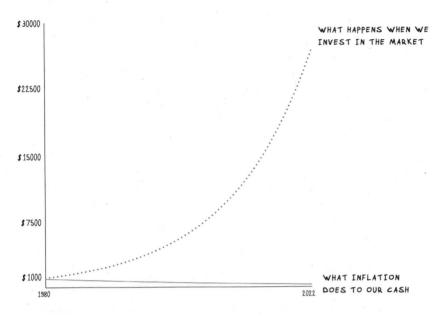

Figure 1: The difference between positive compounding in the stock market and the negative compounding due to inflation.

percent per year. If we correct that for inflation, the market returned 8.38 percent a year. It doesn't sound like a lot. But look at the alternative, which is to stay in cash.

For cash holders, this is an ugly picture. Imagine you had put $1,000 under your mattress in 1980. Forty-two years later, in 2022, that money would have a real value of $240. But if you had invested that money into the S&P 500 index, you would have a real (inflation-adjusted) return of $29,632.50. In that time period, we've experienced wars, recessions, natural disasters, political tension, stock market bubbles, interest rate increases, and a severe financial crisis. We also went through a global pandemic, which caused nearly seven million fatalities along with a range of secondary problems like double-digit inflation, supply-chain issues, and a labor shortage. And all the while, asset prices went up. The problem is that not everyone owns assets. That causes the wealth gap.

Pretty much every country across the globe, no matter how developed, has a problem with rising inequality. For example, the wealthiest and most prosperous nation in the world, America, has seen the wealth gap between its richest and poorest families double from 1989 to 2016.

It's no wonder economic inequality has captured the attention of politicians and economists for the past few decades. But despite this, not much has changed, because the majority of people are focusing on increasing their salaries. While earning more might give you immediate financial relief, it's not the path to long-term wealth. Data show that for the 99 percent of taxpayers making less than $500,000, salaries and wages account for 75 percent of their income. For millionaires, their salaries only account for 15 percent to 50 percent of their income.

So here's what we know about getting rich: invest your money in reliable assets, and let it grow over time. It sounds so easy, and yet it's one of the hardest things to accomplish in life. Because we don't just want to get rich at all costs. We want more money, but we also want peace of mind at the same time. Those two things don't always go together. You can have so much money you never have to worry about paying the bills and still be terrorized by anxiety about losing that money.

We should prosper financially and mentally. When your finances are solid while your mind is peaceful, that's true wealth. When you no longer solely rely on working to earn money, when your money compounds on its own in the stock market, that's when you can finally liberate yourself from the trap of exchanging your time for money.

While the economy keeps growing despite cataclysmic

events and, as a result, the market keeps going up, there are a few challenges when it comes to successful long-term investing.

Challenge #1: Volatility

Many of us recognize that having exposure to the stock market is a good way to build wealth. The problem is that investing in stocks is difficult because the market is so volatile. Prices constantly go up and down, which plays into two powerful human emotions: fear and greed. We feel fear when the market is going down. We get greedy when the markets start going up and feel the urge to pour our life savings into the market at once.

This dynamic has been magnified in public markets since 2020. Since the COVID-19 pandemic, trading stocks has become more popular than ever. In 2011, individual investors made up a little over 10 percent of total trading volumes in the stock market. By the first quarter of 2021, it was nearly 25 percent.

But markets have been more treacherous. One way to measure volatility is by assessing how often the S&P 500 makes at least a 1 percent move in either direction within a single day. In 2022, the frequency of such swings for the S&P 500 had been more than 87 percent of trading days, a rate previously observed only during the height of the global financial crisis of 2008. Another measure, the CBOE Volatility Index (or VIX), which measures the market's expectation of near-term volatility, has remained elevated from February 2020 all the way through early 2023.

All of this is to say: volatility is high, which makes the market seem erratic. If you try to react to the daily changes in stock prices, either you will lose money or you will stay on the sidelines. You will be successful if you maintain composure in spite of the fluctuating nature of the market.

Challenge #2: Consistency

Picking the right investment strategy is hard. You have literally hundreds of thousands of options to invest your money. Most stockbrokers offer the ability to buy stocks and commodities from all over the world. As I'm writing this, there are more than fifty-nine thousand companies worldwide that you can invest in. Then there are countless other investment vehicles, like ETFs, mutual funds, bonds, and commodities such as gold, silver, copper, and cryptocurrencies.

What's more, there are thousands of "experts" who predict all kinds of events in the economy. There are people on social media who have been warning for a decade of a total collapse of the dollar. Our world is getting faster, louder, and more chaotic, which is only overwhelming us. We can't distinguish what matters from what doesn't and what's true from what's not.

And if we do try to invest in something, we're distracted by the next best thing that comes our way. We try too many different types of strategies, which prevents us from ever being consistent. Successful investing comes down to tuning out irrelevant information, having the strength to stick to your strategy, and resisting the urge to follow other opportunities.

Challenge #3: Prior Losses

Losing money in the stock market is common. Studies that look into the success rates of those individual investors who are highly active show that only between 1 percent and 3 percent make money in the short term. It's hard to imagine that up to 99 percent of all traders lose money, but I'm not surprised. Every person I've spoken to who ever tried their hand at buying and selling stocks has lost money.

Trading stocks for short-term profit always *sounds* great (who doesn't want to make money with a few clicks on their stock-trading app?), but by the time people find out the odds are stacked against them, they have probably already lost enough money that they are fed up with stocks.

What about the pros? About 80 percent of professional money managers underperform the S&P 500 index. This is why so many people have a bad experience with investing. The odds are you've lost money by investing too. And I know from personal experience that when you get burned in the market, you would rather stay away. But you also realize you're missing out on free money. That's essentially what investing in stocks comes down to: putting your money into the market and waiting until you get rich.

Why Managing Your Emotions Is the Key to Investing Success

I always believed that investing was an intellectual puzzle. I thought, *If only I had the right formula*, as if investing were like a math equation you could solve. I was not the only one. In the year 2021 alone, more than eighty million books were sold in the business and money category. Many of these books cover the rational aspects of investing. They teach you a methodology for investing. This is what makes so many of us think that investing is just a matter of learning how to do it from a practical point of view. The truth is that professionals know that investing is not about theory or knowledge; it's about managing your emotions.

Benjamin Graham, who created the first systematic approach to investing in the 1930s, said: "Individuals who cannot master their emotions are ill-suited to profit from the investment process."

This stands in stark contrast to popular belief. The movie *Pi*, released in 1998, best captures the idea that millions of us have about investing. The movie follows a world-class mathematician named Max Cohen, who tries to uncover numerical patterns behind the stock market so he can predict its direction. But no matter how much effort he puts into his pursuit, he can't find a way to predict the market, which drives him insane. Max eventually destroys all his work and gives up. Max's pursuit is something many of us have experienced in a less dramatic way. We start to invest by listening to advice from the news or social media, lose our money, get emotional, and decide that investing is only for Wall Street professionals. I experienced that during the 2008 stock market crash, which wiped out $10 trillion of wealth in America.

I thought that more knowledge about investing and finance would help me to avoid losses. In addition to getting my degrees, I studied the strategies of successful investors. I learned about value investors like Warren Buffett, Charlie Munger, Peter Lynch, Bill Ackman, Geraldine Weiss, Joel Greenblatt, and more. These investors have a long-term strategy that's mostly focused on picking good-quality companies to invest in. But to expand my range of stock market knowledge, I also studied traders like Jesse Livermore, Martin S. Schwartz, Martin Zweig, Paul Tudor Jones, and many others. This side of finance is different from investing. Traders are more concerned with generating a short-term profit by benefiting from price differences. They buy an asset intending to sell it at a higher price. They are not always interested in the underlying value of the asset, as long as it's going up.

But it wasn't until 2017 that I finally figured out the *real* key to investing success, ten years after I bought my first stocks. After all this effort to educate myself, to master the principles of investing, I was still too afraid to actually risk my own money in the market. Every few years I would invest in some stocks, but I never found a way to be consistent. I felt like Max Cohen in *Pi*. I just wanted to give up. Because no matter how much knowledge I gained, I still had nothing to show for it. I'd love to tell you that I turned to philosophy out of curiosity, but it was out of necessity. My pursuit of wealth was leading nowhere, and I felt I had to protect my sanity. One day I was reading Seneca, one of the most prominent Stoics, when I finally understood why I had stopped investing and never gotten back in. Seneca wrote:

> *Every emotion is weak at first, then it rouses itself and gathers strength as it advances; it is more easily kept out than driven out. Who denies that all emotions originate in a natural beginning? Nature has entrusted us with care for ourselves, but when you indulge in it too much, it is a fault.*

I had let my emotions gather strength over the years. Eventually the fear of losing money in the market had become so fierce that it paralyzed me. And I was looking for the wrong cure. I thought that more knowledge could help me to make money, but what I truly needed was care for myself, as Seneca said. I had to stop indulging in my emotions. Everything started to click. It felt like I had an entirely different perspective on an old topic. It was like looking at a problem from a new angle. For years I had been stuck in the trenches. Now I was in a helicopter looking down and seeing the complete picture. I realized:

1. To build wealth in the stock market, I need to master my emotions.
2. To master my emotions, I can use Stoicism.
3. Then I can apply Stoicism to my investing strategy so I master my emotions in the stock market.
4. When I do that, I can be consistent and let my money compound over time.

After my eureka moment, I was eager to learn more. Surely someone had written about how you can use Stoicism to become a better investor. But it didn't seem like anyone had—so I started to document my own journey as a Stoic investor.

In July 2015, I started publishing a newsletter and articles about philosophy, careers, personal finance, and business at dariusforoux.com. I've published over five hundred articles, which have been read by more than thirty million people ranging from C-level executives at Fortune 500 companies to professional athletes. My work has been featured in publications like *Forbes, Entrepreneur, Business Insider,* and *The Economist.* In 2020, the publishing platform Medium commissioned me to write a weekly column about Stoicism, which has attracted more than 275,000 followers.

I had studied and written about both Stoicism and investing separately for years, but it wasn't until February 2021 that I publicly wrote about the two topics combined. I had been secretly putting my Stoic investing strategy to the test for *years.* Once I started to invest by Stoic principles, I instantly saw the benefits in the form of mental fortitude and positive returns on my stock portfolio. My big test came in March 2020, when the S&P 500 dropped 34 percent in a month. My old self would've been scared out of his mind and sold at the bottom. My Stoic self just kept calmly investing. I was certain this strategy was working, and I knew it was time to share what I had learned. That's when I started working on an article with the title of the book that you're now reading. In the article, I briefly introduced the idea of the Stoic Path to Wealth. I was immediately flooded with emails and messages from readers who wanted more. I knew I needed to write that book we were looking for.

· 2 ·

Build Wealth by Applying Ancient Wisdom

Stoicism is a philosophical school of thought founded by Zeno of Citium in Athens, in the third century BC. Zeno came from a wealthy merchant family in Citium, a Phoenician city located on the island known today as Cyprus, and he followed in his father's footsteps to become a merchant. On what seemed like a normal voyage to sell goods, he got shipwrecked off the coast of Athens, losing all his cargo. Zeno lost a fortune that day.

He decided to go to Athens, where he found a book that described Socrates and his life. Zeno asked the bookseller, "Where can I find a man like that?" At that moment, an Athenian philosopher named Crates happened to be walking by the store. The bookseller simply pointed toward the man—*that's your guy*. And that's how Stoicism was born. Zeno experienced loss, tried to find answers in a bookstore, found philosophy, and immediately wanted to learn more. Isn't that how all of us discover philosophy? That's all it is: the pursuit to address one's pain, all to find inner peace.

Stoicism spread from one teacher to another and slowly grew in popularity throughout Greece and Rome. It was a useful philosophy to help navigate the political unrest, conflict, and civil war that abounded. While our world is very different from ancient Rome, Stoicism's lessons remain relevant. Its simplicity and usefulness are why it has stayed alive through the centuries after Zeno.

The foundation of Stoicism is the principle of knowing what you can control and what you can't. The truth is that we control only our actions, beliefs, and judgments. We have no control over external things like other people's opinions, the economy, aging, accidents, and even the outcomes of our decisions. And yet we insist on obsessing and worrying about these things that we don't control, which is exactly why so many of us struggle mentally and financially.

By simply focusing our energy on what we control and not worrying about what we don't control, we can attain inner tranquility. A Stoic person always has an edge in volatile situations. When others lose their temper or succumb to their emotions at the slightest setback, the Stoic always remains calm and looks at the facts. But Stoicism is not about controlling what happens to you; it's about controlling how you *respond* to what happens. The goal is to live in the present moment, free of worries about the things you can't control.

Introducing the Four Most Prominent Stoics

I will introduce you to the ideas of the Stoics through a financial lens in a way that will make sense whether you're a seasoned student of Stoicism or a novice. Throughout this book I will quote the most prominent Stoic philosophers. Let me introduce them to you briefly so you have a better understanding of who they were.

Introducing the Stoics		
WHO	**WHEN**	**WHAT THEY STRESSED**
Lucius Annaeus Seneca	(c. 4 BC–AD 65)	Attaining true freedom by practicing nonattachment to one's wealth
Gaius Musonius Rufus	(c. AD 30–c. 101)	The importance of simple and frugal living as a way to strengthen one's character
Epictetus	(AD 55–c. 135)	Radical acceptance of things one cannot control and a focus on improving oneself
Marcus Aurelius	(AD 121–180)	The importance of fairness and honesty in dealing with others

Lucius Annaeus Seneca was a Roman statesman and philosopher born around 4 BC. He was born into wealth and had a successful career in politics. In his fifties, he withdrew from public life to write philosophical works. He was later implicated in a conspiracy against Emperor Nero and was forced to commit suicide in AD 65.

Gaius Musonius Rufus, born around AD 30, was a Stoic philosopher who was born into wealth. He spent his life teaching philosophy instead of pursuing a career in politics like his father. He valued the practice of philosophical exercises and living a frugal lifestyle for self-improvement. Musonius was inspired by the early Stoics, and the school where he taught philosophy was highly respected.

Epictetus, born around AD 55 in Greece to an enslaved mother, attended classes taught by philosopher Musonius before being freed from slavery and teaching Stoicism in Rome. He later founded his own school in Nicopolis, Greece, and emphasized the importance of accepting anything that happens to us without being defined by external factors. His student Arrian recorded Epictetus's teachings and published them as *Discourses* and *Enchiridion*.

Marcus Aurelius was born in AD 121 and became co-emperor of Rome at nineteen. He expanded Roman rule to encompass Germania and Raetia. These territories include the modern-day countries of Germany, Austria, and Switzerland, as well as parts of the Netherlands, Belgium, and France, which essentially meant he ruled almost the entire continent of Europe. Aurelius learned about Stoicism from Epictetus, whose teachings he quoted in his only published work, *Meditations*. It consists of personal reflections and philosophical insights that Marcus Aurelius wrote during his most stressful time as emperor. Rather than being a formal discourse on Stoicism, it is an intimate look into the thoughts and ideas of a man striving to understand himself, the world around him, and how to live a virtuous life.

Merging Stoicism with Investing

At its core, Stoicism is a survival strategy. Stoicism is not just a set of beliefs; it is a way of protecting your sanity. But you can also apply Stoicism to protect your money. Most people, however, assume that the Stoics had an aversion to money. After all, earning and losing money is something that's not fully within our control. According to traditional Stoicism, the only things that are within our control are our actions and judgments.

Following that logic, we could say that because money does not fall within our control, it's bad. But here's what Epictetus, one of the most stringent Stoics, said about money: "If you can make money remaining honest, trustworthy, and dignified, by all means do it. But you don't have to make money if you have to compromise your integrity." I love this mindset because it doesn't judge those with ambitions of having money.

Want to get rich? Go after it. And if you don't get rich? No problem. Simply focus on doing the right thing and forget about the outcome.

The idea is that good behavior leads to a good life, a life of contribution, loving relationships, and peace of mind. The Stoics were investors. They gave up instant gratification and bad habits to increase their odds of living a peaceful life. That's exactly the key: to find financial fulfillment is to invest in yourself. You part ways with some of your money today so it compounds and you have more of it in the future.

The challenges we face with volatility, consistency, and prior losses stem from an inability to stay levelheaded. After all, who doesn't want to compound their money? The problem is that we let our emotions take control of our decisions. We talk ourselves out of investing and make financial decisions that are not in our best interests.

When you let your investing decisions be guided by Stoicism, you will be the master of your emotions and, in turn, your finances. You will develop an edge that will sow the seeds of long-lasting wealth in the stock market.

· 3 ·

How to Build a Stoic Edge
in Three Steps

very investor who has found success in the market has
had some sort of advantage: an *edge*. Having an edge
means you have something, be it information, skills, or
strategies, that gives you an advantage over every other investor in the world. Before I propose a solid and proven edge to
you in this book, let's briefly look at four common types of
advantages that successful investors have had.

1. **The information edge:** By researching a company
   and industry thoroughly, you can get a good
   understanding of that company's competitive
   position in the market. The more information you
   can acquire and consume about any given company,
   the better investment decisions you can make. And
   you don't need to rely only on investment analysis
   done by others. If you're considering investing in an
   ice cream company, you can do your own surveys
   and research into the company's products. Acquiring
   an information edge is harder than most people
   assume. You need to draw new conclusions from
   the information publicly available, which can take

hours of analysis and requires a comprehensive understanding of investment theories. The positive is that information is freely available, which makes the information edge attainable in theory.

2. **The quant edge:** In the late 1960s, former math professor Edward Thorp started a hedge fund that was different from everyone else's. Thorp used quantitative analysis to beat the market for nearly every year of his fund's existence. The funds that use such strategies are now called "quants," and they use complex math to make trading systems. These funds employ PhDs from all fields with one goal in mind: use math to get an advantage in the market. The mathematical skills required to create a quant edge are immense, making it the least accessible edge.

3. **The size edge:** To the outside world, Warren Buffett is known as the most successful investor in history. To insiders and people who've studied his life, he's an insurance man who invested the premiums of his customers. Buffett built his wealth through an investment vehicle called Berkshire Hathaway, a former textile company that also serves as a holding company. Among its holdings are insurance companies like GEICO, Gen Re, MedPro Group, and eleven more. Warren Buffett and Berkshire made exceptionally smart decisions with all the premiums people paid to their insurance companies. Because they had access to so much extra capital, they could buy a lot of companies outright with the cash at their disposal. You can do that only if you are a large financial player. The idea of a size edge is very simple, but it's hard to obtain because very few people have access to enormous sums of cash.

4. **The Stoic Edge:** Personal investing is done by humans. Even if we decide to make use of AI or a robo-adviser to develop an investment strategy, we make the final calls. And human decision-making is often flawed because our emotions are at play. An investor who manages their emotions and doesn't make any common mistakes automatically has an advantage over the investors who don't have that ability. I call that the Stoic Edge, and all the successful investors I've studied possess that edge. After all, it's impossible to stay wealthy by making too many mistakes and losing money. Unlike the information edge, the quant edge, and the size edge, the Stoic Edge is attainable for every investor and easily grasped.

These advantages are not mutually exclusive. An investor like Warren Buffett has multiple edges. He has an information edge because he spends an average of five hours a day reading everything from newspapers to annual reports on the companies he's interested in. Through his reading, he examines companies that most people overlook. It also happens that Buffett is the biggest investor in the world, often having more than $100 billion in *cash* alone. But he doesn't have only a size and information advantage; he also has the most admirable Stoic Edge in the world of investing. Dozens of books are dedicated to dissecting Warren Buffett's investing strategy and behavior. The goal of these books is to look at what makes him successful so we can copy that behavior. But what those books miss is that the average investor lacks all the advantages that Buffett has. It's difficult to have one advantage in the market, let alone three. That's why most people who read about successful investors don't become wealthy in the market unless they have an edge.

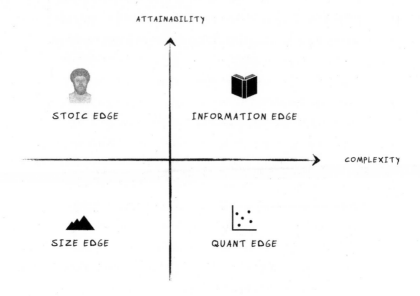

Figure 2: The Stoic Edge ranks high in attainability and low in complexity. That makes it the ideal edge for all investors.

Three Steps to Build a Stoic Edge

The edge of a Stoic is their indifference to everything that's outside their control. If you look at day-to-day situations, you'll see that we waste a lot of emotional energy by responding to things we don't control. Getting angry because there's traffic is a waste of your energy. Looking at your portfolio during a stock market crash is equally fruitless. What matters isn't what happens to us; it's how we *respond*.

Here's my proposition: To build long-term wealth in the stock market, you need to invest throughout your lifetime, no matter what's going on. To be so consistent that you keep investing in spite of feelings like fear and greed, you need to develop the only edge that's accessible to all investors: the Stoic

Edge. When you possess that edge, you will have the mental fortitude to stick to your investing strategy, which will make you wealthier over time.

No matter what type of investing strategy you currently follow, you will benefit from adopting a Stoic Edge. If you're a value or growth investor, the Stoic Edge helps you to avoid selling your stocks during a time when you should be staying the course. If you're a momentum trader, the framework of this book helps you to remove the slightest bit of hesitation or conflict from your trades.

What if you don't have an investing strategy? You're not alone. A survey showed that half of the Americans who want to invest in stocks don't know where to start. Based on the research and experience of the smartest investors in history, there is one strategy that gets recommended repeatedly. It's a strategy that provides good returns and has a proven track record since the 1920s, namely, passive investing in an exchange-traded fund (ETF) that tracks the S&P 500 index.

An ETF gives you exposure to a basket of stocks or other securities without your having to purchase them individually. ETFs are issued by investment companies such as BlackRock, Vanguard, and Fidelity, which then go out and buy each of the stocks in that basket. The ETFs trade on a public exchange and can be purchased through a stockbroker. For instance, the Vanguard S&P 500 ETF is highly popular and can be found via any stock-trading app with its ticker symbol (a unique symbol that allows you to identify an asset on an exchange), VOO.

When you invest in an S&P 500 ETF, you instantly invest in the five hundred largest companies across eleven sectors (like health care, technology, real estate, financials, and so forth) in the United States. Why the U.S.? Even if you live in any other country in the world, and are happy living there, you still want to put your money to work in the greatest economy in the world.

This is why I personally invest in the S&P 500, and I recommend this strategy to my family members. The beauty of this strategy is that it takes almost no time to execute and has a proven track record. The S&P 500's return of 11.44 percent a year on average (since 1980) means your money doubles roughly every six years. That doesn't sound like a bad deal to me, considering the fact that it takes virtually no time to invest in the S&P 500. But to make sure you *stick* to that strategy for your entire life, you need a Stoic Edge.

What I've done in this book is extract the most important lessons from Stoicism, apply them to wealth building, and then boil them down to three simple steps that you can easily remember. If you follow this path, you will acquire a Stoic Edge, which will help you to build wealth in the stock market.

The foundation of this book is based on three steps that are backed by Stoicism, namely: (1) investing in yourself, (2) ac-

THE STOIC PATH TO WEALTH

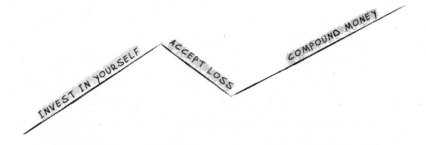

Figure 3: The Stoic path to wealth starts with investing in our skills and earning money. When we can distance ourselves from our money, and accept the idea of potential loss, we can allow it to compound.

cepting loss, and (3) letting your results compound over time. I believe this is the first framework for building a Stoic Edge as an investor. Each step ties into the most important aspect of investing and of Stoicism: managing your emotions. This path might not create overnight millionaires. But it does help you to build wealth.

How This Book Helps You to Build Wealth

While investing philosophies help you to get the best return on your money, Stoicism helps you to get the best return on your *time*. The Stoic Path to Wealth does both. It helps you to build wealth through the stock market while protecting your time and sanity. You'll find a combination of ancient wisdom and practical advice from modern successful investors. I will give you a synthesis of the most useful ideas wise philosophers and investors have already figured out.

Every chapter starts with a profile of an investor. A book about wealth building that doesn't include stories about prolific investors like Warren Buffett, Peter Lynch, John Bogle, and Stanley Druckenmiller would be lacking a huge part of financial history. Even though you might know about these investors, in this book you will uncover new insights about their lives in terms of Stoicism.

In addition to these well-known investors, I also tell the stories of phenomenally successful yet lesser-known people like Geraldine Weiss, Cathie Wood, Jesse Livermore, Edward Thorp, and Mohnish Pabrai. Weiss was the first successful female investor on Wall Street, paving the way for women on Wall Street today. Wood changed the way we look at disruptive companies and short-term financial losses. Livermore was the first famous Wall Street trader who built a booming career out of buying and selling stocks—and young traders still admire his advice from more than one hundred years ago. Thorp was the first to introduce math to investing. Pabrai is the most striking example of an immigrant who built a fortune in the U.S. by executing solid investment advice instead of reinventing the wheel.

I've extracted the lessons from these investors' lives and put them into the terms of Stoic philosophy. The structure of every chapter is as follows: First you'll learn about the defining time of an investor's career, and then I'll show how you can apply those lessons in a Stoic way in your own journey toward building wealth. Every chapter also includes a small segment called "Meditate on this." These are Stoic thought exercises meant to practice your ability to control your emotions.

Finally, at the end of the book, you'll find a section called "Stoic Investing Techniques." This section will answer all your "How should I do this?" questions. If you have an appetite to pick individual stocks or trade options, futures, crypto, and so forth, I will also give you a method for trading that you can use in conjunction with your other, long-term, investment strategy. Even though I'm a long-term investor who invests in the S&P 500 index, I also trade individual stocks and futures. But I pick my trades carefully, cap my losses, and, most important, make sure my trading is profitable.

When it comes to building wealth, it's not about how much you know; it's about how good you are at managing your emotions. The better you manage your emotions, the more consistent you will be. The more consistent you are, the better you can execute your investing strategy, which is what makes you wealthy. This mental aspect of investing is by far the most important part. By the end of this book, you will have that Stoic Edge.

MEDITATE ON THIS . . .

*That things have no hold on the soul.
They stand there unmoving, outside it.
Disturbance comes only from within—
from our own perceptions.*

—Marcus Aurelius

The Stoic dichotomy of control says that we control our actions but not the outcomes of what we do. A person who always eats healthy and exercises can still die from heart disease.

What do we control when it comes to investing? Our strategy and whether we follow through. Form the habit of looking at your actions when you talk about investing. What are you going to do? And how are you going to do it?

Avoid thinking about outcomes. How much will you actually earn with investing? When will you cash out? These outcomes are not within our control, so it's a waste of energy to focus on them in the present moment.

Invest in Yourself

Not to assume it's impossible because you find it hard.
But to recognize that if it's humanly possible,
you can do it too.

—MARCUS AURELIUS

· 4 ·

Valuable Skills Are
Better Than Money

The first step in building wealth isn't about investing in the market, but rather about investing in yourself. The truth is, developing skills is crucial to achieving financial success and stability. Having a solid skill set helps you to provide value in the economy, which empowers you to persevere in the face of any adversity in your career. Your skills become a reliable means of earning money, regardless of market fluctuations. While it's possible to lose money, the skills you've acquired will always remain with you, ready to be utilized for generating income.

From High School Dropout to Making $100 Million

An unlikely place to find a rags-to-riches story is Wall Street. Many professional traders and investment bankers there come from privileged backgrounds, have Ivy League degrees, and were academic standouts. But one of the earliest successes on Wall Street, Jesse Livermore, didn't even finish high school. Today, Livermore is considered the best stock trader of all time.

Born in 1877, Livermore grew up on a farm in Acton, Massachusetts. When he was fourteen years old, his father forced him out of school and ordered him to work on the family farm. But the young Livermore had a passion for reading and math. He hated the idea of following in his father's footsteps; he dreamed of becoming a stock trader because he always read the finance section of the newspaper as a boy. With his mother's help, he escaped to Boston. When he arrived in 1891, he immediately went to the stock brokerage office of Paine Webber. Inside Paine Webber, Livermore found the branch manager and said he wanted a job—any job. He was lucky. The brokerage firm happened to be looking for a "board boy" and Livermore was offered the job on the spot. For the next two and a half years, Livermore worked the boards at Paine Webber. He simply wrote down stock prices on a blackboard, which was the primary way investors could learn the latest prices.

There was no better place to learn how to trade stocks than at a prime stockbroker, and Livermore soaked up everything like a sponge. He had access to experienced brokers, wealthy customers, and the latest stock prices. During downtimes and lunch breaks, the experienced brokers captivated him with their trading theories.

When he came home, he couldn't let go of the market. He kept a journal of the movements of stock prices and started seeing trends. He memorized the movements of a stock, and based on how its price behaved, he made his predictions of what the stock would do next.

To his surprise, Livermore discovered that his predictions were right 70 percent of the time, which gave him enough confidence to pursue a career as a stock trader. His strategy of following trends eventually laid the foundation for a trading method we call "technical analysis" today. It relies on deciphering historical patterns of trading data to predict a stock's future movement.

Livermore had saved up almost $200 that he wanted to use to buy and sell stocks. However, at that time investors had to pay hefty commissions to brokers in addition to transaction costs. Because brokers made more commissions on wealthy clients, they weren't interested in small investors like Livermore. As a result, he couldn't open a brokerage with his $200, even though it was a lot of money for a barely sixteen-year-old kid in the nineteenth century.

But Livermore was determined to get in on the stock market, so he settled on the next best thing: bucket shops. Trading in a bucket shop was more like betting on a horse race. The shops displayed the latest stock prices and people bet on which share would go up or down. None of their money ever went to buying the actual stock.

It was the only place for Livermore to apply his skills. And he was immediately successful, making over $50 a week. Livermore kept winning, which gave him enough confidence to quit his job at Paine Webber when he was seventeen so he could pursue stock trading full time.

But bucket shops, like casinos, made money only when most of their customers were losing. And unlike other customers, Livermore kept on winning, which alarmed the bucket shops. His luck finally ran out when he kept racking up profits at a single shop, totaling $10,000 over the course of many trades. The shop, which was operated by a family with ties to the Mafia, had had enough of Livermore and banned him.

By this time, the other bucket shop owners in Boston had heard about Livermore's track record and didn't want him to set foot in their establishments. Livermore, determined to keep trading stocks, decided to move from Boston to New York. But when he arrived in September 1900 with a bag full of money and confidence from his success, he found that New York bucket shops were closing.

The popularity of bucket shops threatened the business of Wall Street, which operated on costs and commissions. At one point, the size and scale of trading done in bucket shops exceeded those at the New York Stock Exchange, meaning that the legitimate businesses were missing out on profit. Because bucket shops were also used to launder money, authorities targeted them and started to close them.

The decline in bucket shops changed nothing for Livermore because he figured that the same system he used to trade in bucket shops would also work at brokerages. By this point, the twenty-three-year-old Livermore had six years of full-time trading experience, and he had enough money to open a brokerage account.

When Livermore started trading in New York, a new bull market had just started. In a bull market, prices go up fast, fueled by the excitement of a large crowd of investors. There were weeks when Livermore racked up thousands of dollars on every trade. In one of his most memorable early trades, he turned $10,000 into $50,000 in less than a week.

It was Livermore's first taste of a bull market, and he enjoyed his wealth by going on his first proper vacation, which he spent in Europe. But he was always a skeptical person. He had had a hard childhood, growing up on a farm on the unforgiving soil of Massachusetts. Livermore knew that just like seasons, bull markets also come to an end.

In 1907 he began to sell short Union Pacific and Reading Railroad, among other large public companies. Selling a stock short means you're betting against it, borrowing shares and then selling them, with hopes of buying them back for less later and profiting from the difference.

Soon after Livermore shorted the stocks, the Panic of 1907 broke out, caused by excessive stock speculation driven by loose monetary policy. It was a severe financial crisis that shook the U.S. In mid-October, the New York Stock Exchange saw a severe drop of almost 50 percent from its highest point in the previous year.

Livermore made $1 million in the panic. But his success didn't last long. Less than a year later, he lost his entire fortune on a trade where he bet against the price of cotton. The exact opposite of what he expected happened. He lost his entire fortune on one trade and declared bankruptcy that year. He returned to his journals, filled with the strategies that had brought him so much success, this time to reflect on his mistakes. After his bankruptcy he made a breakthrough. He said, "I don't have to beat Wall Street. I have to beat myself, my emotions."

While he felt like he had improved as an investor, it wouldn't be the last time he lost money in the market. In 1915 he went bankrupt again. But no matter how much he lost, he always believed in his ability to earn money with stocks. During his time on Wall Street, he had built an extensive network of people in banks and brokerage firms who also believed in his ability to make money for them. After all, those firms profited every time Livermore traded.

Despite Livermore's increasing debts leading up to both of his bankruptcies, the brokerages didn't press him for repayment. They knew that Livermore's fortune wasn't built on luck. If someone loses their money but regains all of it and more—and they do that multiple times—it's a testament to that person's skill.

His reputation ensured that he had access to capital, which is the most important thing a professional trader needs. By the end of 1916, his net worth was back up to a staggering

$3 million after winning big on several trades. From that point on, he steadily kept growing his wealth and reputation on Wall Street every year. That reputation was set in stone when the stock market crashed in 1929 and most investors lost their fortunes; Livermore, on the contrary, came out on top.

October 28, 1929, is now known as "Black Monday." Prices on the New York Stock Exchange dropped by nearly 13 percent in a single day, which was unprecedented. Worse, the following day was "Black Tuesday," when the market crashed another 12 percent. In two days, billions of dollars were lost and thousands of investors got wiped out.

When Livermore went home that day, his wife and children quickly rushed to him with tears in their eyes. His then wife, Dorothy Livermore, had been sitting by the radio all day, listening to the news reports about high-flying investors who had now suddenly gone broke. She was preparing the children to absorb the shock that they might soon move out of their mansion, sell all their valuables, and live in a modest apartment in a cheaper part of the city.

But instead, Livermore greeted them with a smile. He was on the right side of that crash. He had been short selling for much of 1929, and when the market took a dive on that fateful Monday, he celebrated. Livermore pocketed $100 million ($1.5 billion in today's dollars) in a matter of days. Throughout his career, regardless of the wins and losses, Livermore remained committed to learning and refining his skills. When the most significant opportunity of his life emerged in the form of a stock market crash, he was well prepared to seize the moment and capitalize on it.

How to Learn Faster with the Skill Springboard

Zeno believed that "the goal of life is to live in harmony with nature." Simply put, it means those who adapt themselves to the world are happy, and those who don't are not. This is also the key to career success. If we look for the answers within, we will thrive in the world. If we ask ourselves, *How can I provide value to society?* and then acquire the skills to do that, we will always have work. This ability to adapt is like a money-printing machine.

Jesse Livermore's upbringing is in stark contrast to how Zeno grew up. And yet they had the same approach to life. They both adapted *themselves* to the world and didn't ask the world to adapt to them. Isn't the latter a formula for frustration? If we expect that we should be guaranteed a job simply because we have a degree, we will soon learn a lesson in humility. We live in a transactional economy. You create value, and in return you're financially rewarded.

The foundation for building wealth from nothing is to acquire skills that increase your value in society. Any skill that gives you the opportunity to generate income is valuable. Think of writing, coding, public speaking, designing, or leading. Think of the concept of valuable skills as fluid. Knowing how to modify a telegraph to communicate stock prices might have been a valuable skill in the nineteenth century. But it became obsolete once the telephone and later the fax machine were introduced. If you want to be someone who can adapt yourself to the world, you must learn how to learn. When you're able to acquire any skill, you can adapt to what the world needs. Robert Greene, the author of *Mastery*, a book about the importance of skill development in a person's life, said it best: "The future belongs to those who learn more skills and combine them in creative ways."

Stoics took pride in their ability to adapt. They could always find inner peace no matter what life threw at them. This fluid mindset is essential in today's world, where new technology arrives and changes faster than ever.

We must train ourselves to become learning machines, to adapt to any situation. As Epictetus said: "What then is education? Education is the learning how to adapt."

The Stoics and the most successful investors indeed have a unique approach to learning. I call this framework the Skill Springboard.

1. **Work with your natural abilities:** Every person has inherent strengths. You will be able to provide more value if you focus on what you're already good at.
2. **Learn from the best:** If you decide to learn anything, commit to only learning from the best. By studying the greats, it's more likely you will get to new heights.
3. **Break free from your mentors:** At some point in your progress, you will start to tie everything you've learned together into a unique way of putting your skills to work.
4. **Do your best, but don't overexert yourself:** You must protect your mental health and get enough rest. If you put too much pressure on yourself to succeed, you risk burning out.

This framework will help you to launch or boost your career. Here are the elements described in more detail.

1. WORK WITH YOUR NATURAL ABILITIES.
Nothing can slow down your progress in life more than going against your own nature. Instead of building a career based on our talents, strengths, or interests, we pursue opportunities

for the wrong reasons. Maybe your parents want you to become a lawyer, and you go to law school, only to figure out it's not in line with your natural abilities. Or maybe you get enticed by stories of twenty-something start-up founders who made a fortune in Silicon Valley, which drives you to found your own company, only to figure out you can't stand working for yourself.

As Livermore learned early in his life, we're better off if we pursue the things that we're passionate about and that we're good at. Young Livermore faced pressure to follow in his father's footsteps as a farmer, but he loved reading about finance. In addition to that, he was good at math.

To become excellent at a skill, we need both things: passion and natural ability. There must be some kind of talent or natural ability that makes performing a skill relatively easy for you.

When we try to acquire a skill just because it gives us the potential to earn a higher salary or because it's popular, even though we have no natural talent at it, we quickly learn we're pursuing something fruitless. What matters is that we focus on ourselves and avoid pursuing opportunities that are not in line with our interests and abilities. It made sense for Livermore to pursue a career as a stockbroker given his passion, math skill, and excellent memory, which only improved as he got older.

Honing skills at the intersection of interest and ability also requires a certain amount of self-reflection, which is an important aspect of Stoicism. Seneca, one of the wealthiest Stoics, often wrote about how we need to examine ourselves. In his late fifties, Seneca withdrew from public life and devoted his time to writing some of his most notable philosophical works, including 124 letters to his friend Lucilius. Seneca urged his friend to "search yourself and examine and observe yourself in different ways."

Don't expect to know yourself without making an effort. Like Livermore, keep a journal. Write your thoughts on paper. Read your musings and analyze them. Search for clues about what you're good at. Often, those are the things you write about the most.

2. LEARN FROM THE BEST.

"Mastery of reading and writing requires a master," according to the philosopher-king Marcus Aurelius. When he wrote this, he was arguably the most powerful person in the West as the ruler of Rome. Yet he was humble; he didn't feel like he was above other people, and he had a desire to learn from the best.

When Jesse Livermore started working at Paine Webber, he was immersed in the world of finance at one of the top brokerages in America. He learned something new during almost every interaction at work, even if it was during the lunch break. This is an undervalued aspect of skill development. I started a company with my father in 2010, but after three and a half years, I felt stuck in my development. So I took a job at Gartner, a Fortune 500 company and the leading firm in IT research. I wanted to work for one of the best companies in the world to see how they did things there.

In my time at Gartner, I learned more from spending time at bars and restaurants with my high-performing coworkers outside work hours than I did during the formal two-month training program I received when I started. The more time you spend with people who are great at what they do, the more you pick up on what makes them great.

When you set out to learn new skills, commit to learning only from the best. Don't take advice from people who aren't excellent at what they do. Livermore went to the best stock brokerage for a reason. He wanted to be the best. As Epictetus said: "Now is the time to get serious about living your ideals. . . . Decide to be extraordinary and do what you need to do—now."

3. BREAK FREE FROM YOUR MENTORS.

When you study the best people in any field, you notice how everyone has their own unique way of doing things. Look at successful investors and you'll see that every person has a slightly different stock-picking strategy. These people become your mentors and teachers. Without them you wouldn't be where you are.

But at some point, you must break free from the role of pupil. It's time to take everything you've learned and create your own ideas, style, strategy, code, art, or writing.

When Jesse Livermore quit his job at Paine Webber, he felt confident he could successfully pick stocks. He had learned everything he could from his mentors, clients, and coworkers, and he used it to create his own method for trading stocks.

Epictetus also talked about the importance of breaking away from your mentors: "You're not yet Socrates, but you can still live as if you want to be him." Even though you might not yet be at the top of your field, always carry yourself as someone who has the *desire* to be singular.

I've also experienced this path as a writer. A common piece of writing advice is to start by copying your favorite authors. The famous journalist, writer, and teacher William Zinsser wrote an essay called "Looking for a Model" where he said: "Writing is learned by imitation; we all need models." When I started, my models were Hemingway, Palahniuk, and Zinsser himself. Copying my favorite writers helped me to get started. You will find that many writers start out that way. But one thing a lot of writers don't get is that Zinsser stressed that you must look for a model *when you start*. This is also what Zinsser stressed in his 1976 bestselling book *On Writing Well*, which is still considered essential reading for writers. As a writer you eventually need to develop your own unique style, because who cares about reading the nth Hemingway wannabe?

At some point you've learned enough. Stop following others. Start doing things your way.

4. DO YOUR BEST, BUT DON'T OVEREXERT YOURSELF.

To be great, you need to consistently learn and practice, which takes a lot of energy. While it may be tempting to press on no matter what, it's important to recognize when we are reaching our limit. It's impossible to remain Stoic without carefully tending to our personal energy. When we're overtired and burned out, that becomes apparent in every area of our lives, whether it's at work, at home, or in our investment decisions.

To perform well, we must understand when to take a step back. Knowing one's limits was something that Jesse Livermore, sadly, didn't live by. Between 1900 and 1934, he went bankrupt three times. His bankruptcies followed the same pattern every time. He took too much risk and tried too hard to make a lot of money. He played only to hit a home run. He

Figure 4: View your personal energy as a speedometer. You could go into "the red" if you wanted to. But pushing yourself too hard can be detrimental in the long run, as it can lead to burnout. To be consistent and do your best, get enough rest, and dedicate time to mental recovery.

was obsessed with trading and would even abruptly end his vacations to get back to his work.

Because he had his skills and experience to rely on, he won back millions after every bankruptcy—except the last one, in 1934. Livermore was exhausted from the ups and downs. He felt like a stranger on Wall Street, which was more regulated than before the Great Depression. His investments stopped succeeding, which drove him to write books about investing. But after several years of writing and after publishing two books, he started to sink into a depression that he never got out of. Tragically, he took his own life in 1940, at the age of sixty-three.

Depression is a serious issue that requires professional help from mental health specialists; we must raise awareness and practice understanding for those suffering from mental illness. One way we can improve our own mental health is by avoiding overexerting ourselves. That's difficult, because so many of us tend to put too much pressure on ourselves to succeed in our careers. We want everything to happen fast.

Stoic philosophy reminds us to let go of that pressure, take a step back, and focus on the things we control. When it comes to our careers, we can control only how well we perform and what we offer to the world. We don't control the monetary rewards we get. This is why the foundation of wealth building starts with developing our skills. It's the thing we have 100 percent control over.

MEDITATE ON THIS . . .

Only the educated are free.

—Epictetus

What's your view of education? The majority of the population looks at education as the first part of a person's life; when you're out of school, you're done with education.

But are we really ever done getting educated? Look at it this way. As long as you keep educating yourself, you will be free.

When the Stoics talked about freedom, they didn't talk only about financial freedom. Freedom in a Stoic sense means liberation from ignorance. It means the freedom to live your life peacefully. To not get attached to ideas and beliefs. To not get swayed by external events. And to have tranquility at all times.

We can obtain those things by continuously sharpening our minds.

• CHAPTER SUMMARY •

- Focus on your skills at the start of your journey toward building wealth. When you know how to acquire skills, you will be able to adapt to life and the economy. When you have valuable skills, you will not be long without a job.
- Live in agreement with the laws of human nature. To live well is to live in harmony with the facts of life. That means trying to fit in and not resisting the things we can't change.
- Use the Skill Springboard to learn faster. Focus on the skills you're naturally good at and aim to become great. Learn from the best. Develop your own unique way of doing things. And give every day your best effort.

- Protect your mental health. Play the long game by making sure you can stay productive and consistent. You make more progress when you do your best for a long time than when you overexert yourself briefly and then recover.

· 5 ·

The Hidden Principles
of the Market

Everyone perks up at the idea of a shortcut to wealth. Everywhere on the internet, you'll find advice and schemes to get rich quick. But none of the prominent investors you'll read about in this book have taken shortcuts. They all started from the bottom of the ladder and climbed up. They learned the basics of investing before they started growing their wealth. After reading this chapter, you will have a solid understanding of the factors that drive the stock market, a grasp of the investment industry, and the know-how to invest wisely. This knowledge removes any uncertainty and mystery about investing. You will know what you're doing.

Learning Everything about the
Business of Investing

In the spring of 1950, a nineteen-year-old Warren Buffett got the idea to apply to Harvard Business School. He was close to finishing college in his hometown at the University of Nebraska, and he wanted to pursue his education at Harvard.

He felt like he needed the prestige and network of an Ivy League university. When he showed up at the interview, he quickly realized that wasn't going to happen: "I looked about sixteen and emotionally was about nine. I spent ten minutes with the Harvard alumnus who was doing the interview, and he assessed my capabilities and turned me down."

But his rejection from Harvard changed his career for the better. Instead, Buffett was accepted at Columbia, where he met his mentor, Benjamin Graham, who cowrote the seminal book *Security Analysis* with colleague David Dodd. Before the 1930s, long-term investing was nonexistent on Wall Street. In fact, from the creation of the stock market in the eighteenth century until the late 1920s, stocks were primarily for speculators.

Traders bought stocks not to build long-term wealth but to make a short-term profit. That strategy of buying and selling became more widespread (and risky) during the Roaring Twenties. At the time, it was almost impossible to lose money with stocks. People bought stocks at high prices and sold them at even higher ones.

One of the first people to propose stocks as a medium for long-term investing was Edgar Lawrence Smith, author of the 1924 book *Common Stocks as Long Term Investments*. In his book, Smith challenged the conventional wisdom that stocks were solely a medium for speculation. He was the first to apply statistical analysis to the investment returns of stocks. Smith found that stocks outperformed bonds for the first two decades of the twentieth century. Looking further back, he found that during any fifteen-year period, there was only a 1 percent chance of suffering a loss if an investor held a broad range of stocks (similar to an index like the Dow Jones Industrial Average). Those data still hold up today.

Graham and Dodd built on this body of work that looked

differently at stocks. In fact, *Security Analysis* became the most important book for investing in the 1930s and much of the twentieth century. Warren Buffett devoured that book, as well as Graham's follow-up book, *The Intelligent Investor*, published in 1949. Both books blew away Wall Street's conventions. Buffett desperately wanted to work with Graham, the man who had launched a revolution on Wall Street and created a long-term and systematic approach to investing.

When Buffett started his degree in economics at Columbia in 1949, he hoped to secure a job at Graham's fund, Graham-Newman Corp. He was an A+ student and forged a relationship with Graham. He even offered to work for Graham for free. But Graham turned him down because the firm hired only Jewish people. At the time, investment banks were anti-Semitic, and Graham-Newman wanted to make a difference. So Buffett moved back to Nebraska to work as a stockbroker at his father's company, Buffett-Falk & Co.

He didn't like his first job at Buffett-Falk, where he had to sell stocks to clients. Buffett liked to buy stocks for himself, but he couldn't stand persuading others to buy. He especially hated it when his stock recommendations ended up losing money for his clients.

Today we can buy mutual funds or index funds that are essentially baskets of stocks. Back then, investors had to pick individual stocks. The popular index funds of today didn't exist. If you wanted to invest, you had to go to your stockbroker for guidance on what to buy, as well as to execute the purchase.

While Buffett wasn't new to investing, he *was* new to the business of investing. Buffett learned there's a difference between investing, as in the skill of investing, and *investing*, as in the business of investing.

The business of investing is an entire industry predicated

on generating revenue on the back of stocks and other securities. For example, when Buffett was a stockbroker, he would get paid based on turnover instead of performance. Whether his clients won or lost, Buffett got paid. This didn't sit well with him.

Buffett famously made his first investment, of $114, in 1941 at the age of eleven. Ten years later, his personal stock portfolio was worth $19,738, and yet he couldn't make a sale at work. "I was twenty-one. And I'd go around to all these people to sell them stocks, and when I'd get all through, they'd say, 'What does your dad think?' I got that all the time," he recalled.

When he found out that some clients listened to his advice but used his ideas to buy the stocks through other brokers, he felt cheated. He was slowly learning the principles of the business of investing, and he didn't like it one bit. He wanted to manage people's money and be left alone.

Like any person who doesn't find fulfillment in their career, Buffett started looking elsewhere. He wanted to break away from the job he had started to hate. If he could have more financial security, he could do what he loved full time: investing in stocks. On a whim, he decided to buy a local gas station with one of his friends, in hopes of earning some money on the side. Buffett was now a small business owner. But it didn't turn out as he expected.

"My service station was the dumbest thing—I lost two thousand dollars, and that was a lot of money for me at the time. I'd never had real damage in a loss. It was painful." He ended up losing 20 percent of his net worth. The station never made any money, primarily because next door there was a Texaco station, which attracted more customers.

Ever since Buffett had gotten back to Omaha, nothing had turned out the way he expected. He was too inexperienced and couldn't find his way. But he made sure to keep in touch with his mentor, Ben Graham. He had learned that he would rather buy stocks with other people's money than be a stockbroker, who lives off commissions. But because he had no opportunity to become a professional investor in Omaha, he kept suggesting stock ideas to Graham. His strategy was to keep making himself useful to Graham. Indeed, Buffett's stocks tips proved to be successful.

After two years of being in touch, Graham wrote and said, "Come on back." Buffett's persistence had paid off. Graham-Newman was a small company with only eight people, including the two partners. When Buffett joined, he sat at a desk in a windowless room and scrupulously researched companies. He looked at financial data, stock prices, and management teams and sometimes even visited the companies if he could. He made a point of doing more research than anyone else.

Other professional investors would sit in their offices and simply read reports that stock analysts wrote. Stock analysts are responsible for researching and evaluating financial data, market trends, and company performance to provide investment recommendations and forecasts.

But Buffett didn't like to rely on someone else's biases and opinions. He went straight to the source to get his data, whether it was the company itself or the SEC. Buffett recalled, "I was the only one who ever showed up at those places. They never even asked if I was a customer. I would get these files that dated back forty or fifty years. They didn't have copy machines, so I'd sit there and scribble all these little notes, this figure and that figure."

Graham's strategy was to find "cigar butt" companies, cheap and discarded stocks whose assets were worth more than the company's price on the public market. The way Graham saw it, you could buy companies at a discount, which he called a "margin of safety." While Buffett's strategy has changed since then, he still lives by the concept of having a margin of safety. When you pay less for an asset than it's worth, it's difficult to lose money.

For two years, Buffett learned the principles of sound investing at a job that he finally loved. And when he was in the office, he kept his ears open about how the business of investing works. Buffett realized he could turn small amounts of money into big lumps with his skills and knowledge. And he didn't have to sell stocks to strangers to accomplish that.

But the professional relationship between Buffett and Graham was never meant to last long. Buffett was at the beginning of his career. Graham was sixty-two years old and was ready to retire. In 1956, Graham decided to close the fund and move to Los Angeles to teach at UCLA.

By that time, Buffett had boosted his personal capital to $140,000 through his investments. When Graham-Newman closed, Buffett once again moved back home. This time he was committed to staying and to starting his own fund, modeled after his mentor's partnership. Buffett didn't only have experience, knowledge, and positive investing returns; he also had built a reputation as a solid investor.

When Graham-Newman closed the fund, its investors asked Ben Graham whom they should hand their money to, to which he replied: "Warren Buffett."

The Three Underlying Principles of the Stock Market

A stock market is simply a place where buyers and sellers of stocks meet. While traditional marketplaces have existed for around five thousand years (the first record of marketplaces and bazaars dates to 3000 BC), stock markets really started to take off in the early seventeenth century. In 1602, the Dutch East India Company issued shares that were made publicly tradable on the Amsterdam Stock Exchange. In theory, any person could become a joint owner of a company by buying a stock certificate. In practice, buying stocks was only for people who were born into wealth.

In a way, that trend remained alive until the twentieth century. Even though it was easier for an individual to buy stocks in the 1950s than in the 1920s, each purchase still came with high transaction costs, especially if you bought stocks with small sums. For example, transactions between $100 and $400 came with a commission of $3 plus 2 percent of the amount traded (with a $6 minimum). The cost of that $100 stock is actually $106. So if you bought $100 worth of stocks, you instantly gave up 6 percent of your returns.

Moreover, there was no real underlying logic to stock markets until the second half of the twentieth century. People simply bought stocks that went up and sold stock that went down. Who knew what the real value of a stock was? With the invention of modern finance, that changed. People like Edgar Lawrence Smith, Benjamin Graham, and Warren Buffett introduced the idea of systematic investing. Over the years, the stock market outgrew its marketplace phase and became a system. I've identified three underlying principles that the system is built on. You can think of these principles like the rules of a game. Through centuries of operating stock markets across the globe, the investing community has established these principles as common truths.

Understanding the underlying principles of the stock market allows you to approach investing with a rational, calm, and informed mindset. This knowledge helps prevent emotional re-

THE THREE UNDERLYING PRINCIPLES
OF THE STOCK MARKET

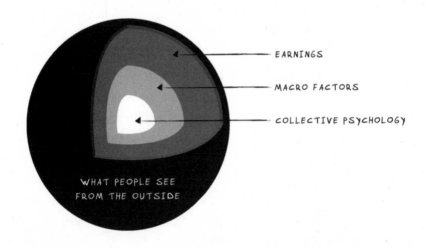

EARNINGS

MACRO FACTORS

COLLECTIVE PSYCHOLOGY

WHAT PEOPLE SEE
FROM THE OUTSIDE

Figure 5: From the outside, the stock market seems mysterious. It seems like markets behave irrationally. But when we look underneath the surface, we find that there are principles that drive the market. When you know about these principles, the stock market no longer seems like a mystery.

actions, such as fear or anxiety, from influencing your investment decisions. When others may be swayed by opinion makers and assume that the market is a mystery, you will have a solid grasp of the fundamental mechanisms driving the market. As a result, you can navigate market fluctuations with confidence and make more informed choices based on the following principles.

1. EARNINGS

The most common platitude in real estate investing is "Location, location, location." While the saying might be banal, it's very true. A decent property in a great location is better than a good property in a bad location. And because we can't build more land, prime locations will always remain in demand. In the stock market, there's a similar saying: "Earnings, earnings, earnings." *Earnings* refers to a company's profits in a given quarter or fiscal year.

When I started investing, I had no idea what moved a stock. I compared it to real estate. I assumed that popular stocks were like properties with great locations. But the problem with stocks is that in the history of the market, no company has remained popular over multiple decades. Apartments close to Central Park in New York City or houses near the beach on the French Riviera were popular a hundred years ago, and they remain popular today. It's safe to assume that in another hundred years, those properties will remain as much in demand as they are now.

You can't say that for stocks. In the 1920s, investors assumed that companies like General Electric (which went public in 1896) would always remain in demand. After all, who could imagine a future where GE wouldn't be one of the biggest companies in the world? People said the same thing about steel companies in the 1950s. No single company remains on top forever. That's because stocks are driven by earnings. When a company grows and earns more, the stock price goes up. A company doesn't even need to post a profit for its stock to go up. If investors see a *promise* of future profit, they are willing to buy a stock today in anticipation of future earnings growth.

The entire professional investing industry is built on the concept of earnings. Institutional investors like mutual funds, hedge funds, pension funds, and insurance companies use investment models that primarily look at earnings. Just as in any industry, there are trends. When Wall Street identifies a stock that has high upside potential, all the pros start to buy its stocks, which drives up the price. When a stock gets attention, stock analysts (who make buy, hold, and sell recommendations) join the party. After a stock sees more buyers and professional coverage by Wall Street insiders, the media latches on. You'll start hearing about the exceptional returns of any particular stock on CNBC, in *The Wall Street Journal*, or on social media. This is when the public starts getting interested in the stock. But what the public doesn't recognize is that the growth story of most companies doesn't last long. This whole scenario could take two years. And all the while, the pros have been riding the stock up. They know everything about the companies they invest in, and they recognize as no one else does that earnings is the only thing that matters.

At the first hint of a slowdown of earnings growth, Wall Street can ditch a stock within a matter of days. That's how these high-flying stocks come down. The earnings of a successful company grow by 30 percent or more, and investors jump on the train in expectation of unusual growth for years to come, but as soon as there's one sign of *normal* growth (up to 10 percent), the stock is dropped. If that company doesn't return to double-digit growth, the stock will not rise again.

This is one of the reasons why the S&P 500 index kept going up over the past decades: it includes only the five hundred public companies in the United States that have the most solid and consistent earnings. The companies that are part of that list are selected by a committee with rigorous standards. If it believes a company is no longer worthy of being part of the S&P 500, it will remove the company and replace it with another company that's doing better. Investors are ruthless when it comes to companies that no longer grow. When the earnings of a company go down, the stock can fall close to zero.

2. MACRO FACTORS

While the ultimate direction of stocks is determined by their growth, the pace of their growth depends on macro factors. The most important factors are, in no particular order, recessions, geopolitics, wars, natural disasters, interest rates, and systemic problems in the financial system (like the financial crisis of 2008). Those elements keep Wall Street operating. Professional investors form narratives about what the stock market will do, and that narrative is largely based on macro factors. Here are the most popular narratives you'll hear in the media.

"A recession is coming. Run!" There are always people who warn of an imminent recession. They make it sound like the next crash will be worse than 1929. A common story is that global growth is slowing down, that governments have too much debt, and that the U.S. dollar is losing strength.

"The Fed will raise interest rates!" The Federal Reserve's goal is to support a healthy economy in the U.S. The primary way it does that is by determining the federal fund rate, which determines at what rates banks can borrow. And that in turn influences market rates like those on your mortgage, car loan, or credit card. Because the economy is dynamic, the Fed needs to decrease and increase the interest rate when necessary. If the economy is overheated, the Fed increases rates. If the economy is slow, it decreases rates.

"Geopolitical events will derail the world economy!" Every year, there's some form of threat to the free world. Yet the stock market has kept going up through wars, pandemics, trade conflicts, natural disasters, different presidential administrations, and so forth.

The media cycle runs on hype and forecasting catastrophe, which influences short-term fluctuations but doesn't stop the long-term growth of the stock market. As a Stoic investor, you understand these narratives and don't react to them.

3. COLLECTIVE PSYCHOLOGY

Investors are highly sensitive to the psychology and mood of other participants in the market. In good times, investors are greedy. They keep pushing prices up, assume that the sky's the limit, and forget about financial history. This is human nature. No one likes to think about winter during the summer. And during the winter, it seems like summer is never coming.

While the stock market behaves rationally over the long term, and it's driven by the underlying principle of earnings, in the short term, the market behaves highly irrationally, driven by investors' collective psychology.

The investor Howard Marks, who has been writing a popular investment memo since 1990, compares short- and intermediate-term stock market behavior, which is driven by collective psychology, to the movement of a pendulum.

Figure 6: The pendulum of market psychology. It represents the swings between the fear and greed of participants. The pendulum is always in motion and never lies still in the middle.

In his book *Mastering the Market Cycle*, Marks writes: "In business, financial and market cycles, most excesses on the upside—and the inevitable reactions to the downside, which also tend to overshoot—are the result of exaggerated swings of the pendulum of psychology." Markets are hardly ever in equilibrium. There's never a time when all investors have a balanced view. Markets operate on the extremes of fear and greed.

What makes investing harder is that these swings in stock prices are often the opposite of what most people expect. For example, a stock might increase in price leading up to the day when the latest earnings of the company are posted. The price is pushed up in anticipation of the news. When the actual earnings are published, the stock price might go down, even when the earnings are great. Why? Wall Street operates on two short-term indicators: anticipation and unexpected news.

When professionals expect something to happen, they will trade as if the thing had already happened. When it happens, they drop the stock and move on to the next trade. This is how many short-term fluctuations are created. The other factor that moves stock prices in the short term is unexpected news. Let's say that the investment community expects that the Federal Reserve will raise interest rates by 0.25 percent, and the Fed suddenly raises them by 0.75 percent. You'll probably see a huge downward movement. Every time the market is truly surprised, you'll see big reactions: upward or downward. The direction is driven by fear and greed. Is there anticipation of something fearful? It'll go down. Do we anticipate something that makes us greedy? It'll go up.

Most investors are not capable of understanding the psychology of the stock market and how it goes back and forth. They fall into herd behavior. They sell when everyone else is selling and buy when everyone else is buying. This results in a "buy high, sell low" strategy, a sure way of destroying your wealth.

Ignore the Stories—Focus on Principles

No industry has more liars and charlatans than finance. These false prophets abuse the common investor's lack of knowledge. Most people start investing in stocks without proper knowledge of how the stock market works. This is not a surprise. Knowledge of the underlying principles of the industry is not important in most fields. Someone can be a great doctor without knowing how the business of health care works. As a writer, I don't know much about the history of the book-publishing industry. You can't say the same for investing in the stock market. Investing in good businesses doesn't always lead to good results, because there are many other factors that determine your success. You can spot a great public company, assess its value, buy the stock for less than it's worth, and still get scared into selling at the first sign of a crash.

This is why common investors and professional traders always need to respect the hidden principles of the stock market: earnings matter in the long term, macro factors determine the swings, and collective psychology oscillates between fear and greed.

The Stoics had this approach to life in general: They always worked with the existing rules, patterns, and principles of society. Their goal was not to change the way life works but to change their own behavior in a way that protected their sanity. No matter what kind of obstacle they faced, they always looked within themselves for the solution. They asked themselves: *What can I change about my behavior or mindset to solve a problem?* As Marcus Aurelius once said: "When jarred, un-avoidably, by circumstance, revert at once to yourself, and don't lose the rhythm more than you can help. You'll have a better grasp of harmony if you keep on going back to it."

Warren Buffett is a master of this mindset. He is notorious for his monk-like lifestyle. He lives close to his office, spends hours a day reading and thinking about investing, has only a few employees, and more than anything, relies on his knowl-edge of the stock market. As a result, he's able to tune out short-term hype—and panic. When the stock market was col-lapsing in the midst of the financial crisis in 2008, Buffett re-mained stoic during the many interviews he gave. He even wrote an opinion piece in *The New York Times* called "Buy American. I Am." In it he wrote, "A simple rule dictates my buying: Be fearful when others are greedy, and be greedy when others are fearful." His message to every investor was to keep investing and stay calm.

No matter what problem you're facing as an investor, the solution is not to walk away. Go back to the fundamental prin-ciples. Make your decision understanding the rules that never change, and don't fall prey to emotions.

MEDITATE ON THIS . . .

Make progress, and, before all else,
endeavour to be consistent with yourself.
And when you would find out whether you
have accomplished anything, consider whether
you desire the same things to-day that you
desired yesterday. A shifting of the will

> *indicates that the mind is at sea, heading in various directions, according to the course of the wind. But that which is settled and solid does not wander from its place.*
>
> —Seneca

Think about a time you started to work toward a goal without doing research. Maybe you tried to learn swimming by watching one YouTube video. Maybe you tried to start a business without taking courses or reading books on entrepreneurship.

When you start that way, you have no idea of what's coming, and that will destroy your odds of success. What's worse, when you don't know what you're doing, it's easy to get fooled by malevolent people.

Every time you set out to do something, commit to finding out the most important principles. Start your endeavor with knowledge. Do as much research as you can. Know where you're going, and the odds are high you will reach your destination.

• **CHAPTER SUMMARY** •

- From the outside, investing looks complex and mysterious. The stock market is not an irrational entity. It only looks irrational in the short term and from the outside.
- The stock market is built on three foundational principles. Earnings, macro factors, and collective psychology determine what the stock market does. In

the short term, it's unstable; in the long run, it's proven to be highly consistent.

- Always keep the principles of investing in mind. It's easy to get caught up in the daily news cycle of the stock market. As a result, we forget what truly moves stocks. If we keep the principles of the stock market in mind, we won't panic over sudden moves in prices. We will stay put.

· 6 ·

Consistency Pays Off:
Investing Is a Habit

nvesting is not something you do occasionally. It's a way of life. When you look at yourself as an investor, your goal is to grow your net worth. It doesn't matter how much your wealth grows every day; what matters is that every day you take the actions that lead to growth. When you consistently invest in yourself, you will see a payoff in every area of your life. First you will see your personal life and career improve. Then your wealth will follow.

The First Lady of Wall Street

On April 1, 1966, a mysterious investor called "G. Weiss" launched an investment newsletter called *Investment Quality Trends*. The newsletter, which still exists today, provided investing insights and strategies for the professional investment community. More than a decade after it started, in 1977, the newsletter caught celebrity investor Louis Rukeyser's attention. He was struck by the fact that *Investment Quality Trends* subscribers consistently achieved excellent returns.

Rukeyser was the host of the TV show *Wall $treet Week with*

Louis Rukeyser and a major investment personality. Getting featured on *Wall $treet Week* was a big deal for investors. At the time, the only major media outlets for the financial community were *The Wall Street Journal, Barron's,* and that show. *Wall $treet Week* featured individuals and companies that achieved outstanding returns in the market. But G. Weiss stood out even among these outstanding investors. When Weiss appeared on *Wall $treet Week,* viewers learned that "G. Weiss" was the pseudonym used by Geraldine Weiss, a fifty-year-old investor and mother of four. G. Weiss was the first famous female investor in the U.S. and became known as the "First Lady of Wall Street."

Weiss decided to use a pseudonym in the 1960s, a period when women were treated with blatant misogyny. Banks could still refuse to issue women credit cards unless their husband was cosigning; pregnancy often resulted in job termination; and even most Ivy League schools accepted only men. (Yale and Princeton didn't accept female students until 1969, and Harvard only started to admit women in 1977.) But to Weiss, it wasn't as bad as her early years.

Weiss was born in 1926 to a Jewish family in San Francisco, and her teenage years were filled with dread from the constant threat of war and anti-Semitism. As she got older, the anti-Semitism gradually worsened until World War II broke out in 1939, when it became downright dangerous to be Jewish. Her father experienced so much discrimination that he decided to change their family name from *Schmulowitz* to *Small* when she was in high school.

Weiss remembered running for a school position once under the name *Schmulowitz* and losing. But the following year, after her father changed the name to *Small,* she tried running again. She won. It was a harsh lesson about perception that she carried with her all her life.

Weiss decided to pursue a degree in business and finance at the University of California, Berkeley. In her spare time she went to the public library and devoured every book on investing. She had found her calling in life.

"After all of my reading," Weiss said later, "it was Benjamin Graham and his books *Security Analysis* and *The Intelligent Investor* that really influenced me more than anything. I realized that it was values that, in the long run, determine price more than anything else." She graduated in 1945, and during her college years, she met her future husband. However, instead of immediately starting her career, she chose to focus on building a family with her spouse, a young naval officer.

While she loved the idea of working in finance and earning a living for herself, she felt pressured to become a housewife. As Weiss said, "the goal for women [at the time] was to get married."

In 1962, at age thirty-six, Weiss finally felt ready to start a career in finance. But she struggled. She later remembered consulting with her husband about taking some of their money to buy stocks. She was hesitant to do it because they didn't have a lot of financial freedom then. Another thing that held her back was the mystery of finance.

Weiss had no experience with investing, but she somehow had to start gaining experience. Looking at Wall Street from the outside is one thing; understanding what happens under the hood is something else. It was a profession dominated by white males who wanted to keep their world closed to outsiders. What did a middle-aged mother know about investing, when the rest of society didn't even think women should handle financial matters?

"We were living hand to mouth," Weiss said. "I was so afraid to do it because I didn't want to lose the family money." But her husband was supportive. When the Cuban missile crisis happened and the stock market went down, Weiss saw her opportunity. All around her, investors were panicking and pulling their money out of the market. But Weiss made her move. When the crisis ended, the market bounced back, and Weiss got a good return in a short time.

"Never is there a better time to buy a stock than when a basically sound company, for whatever reason, temporarily falls out of favor with the investment community," Weiss reflected later. "When bad things happen to good companies, it must be viewed as a buying opportunity rather than a bailout."

Despite the growth of her personal portfolio, Weiss struggled for four years to get a job as a professional investor. She applied to brokerage firms and other Wall Street firms. But every time, she was laughed out of the office or was instead offered a secretarial position, which she turned down.

After years of constant rejection, Weiss realized she would never get into the investing world the traditional way. She refused to "start out" as a secretary in a trading firm, because she knew her investment opinions and insights wouldn't be respected there.

In 1966, at the age of forty, Weiss cofounded *Investment Quality Trends*. Passive investing through ETFs or index funds didn't exist then. If you wanted to invest in stocks, you had to buy the securities of individual companies, which made it hard to build long-term wealth. How did you know what stocks to buy?

Because there was no internet, many investors decided which stocks to buy or sell based on tips from friends and relatives and newspapers like *The Wall Street Journal* and *Barron's*. In the 1960s, mail-to-home investment newsletters became popular because investors were always on the lookout for stock tips.

Investment Quality Trends played into that need. Weiss became the first woman to start a successful investment advisory service in the U.S. Because it was still a male-dominated world, Weiss initially collaborated with her broker to start the newsletter. When they sent out their first newsletters, Weiss and her cofounder, Fred Whitmore, each signed half of the copies that were sent out. The newsletters were identical. But those that were signed "Fred Whitmore" got significant responses from subscribers. The newsletters signed "Geraldine Weiss" didn't yield anywhere near the same response. In the fortieth anniversary edition of *IQ Trends*, published in 2006, Weiss reflected, "I will never forget one of the first responses I received to promotion literature that bore my name. It read, 'I can't imagine myself ever taking investment advice from a woman. Unless you take your advice from a man.' (That letter hung on the wall of my office for many years.)"

It showed Weiss that even the common investor was prejudiced against a woman's investing advice. It was at this point that Weiss remembered an old lesson from high school: perception matters. She made a subtle but significant change. "Geraldine Weiss" turned into "G. Weiss." And the responses started to flood in.

Within a year, Weiss bought out Whitmore and started managing the newsletter on her own. She continued to study the market and provide quality investment insights that her subscribers loved. *Investment Quality Trends* has produced positive annual returns for *decades*. Between 1986 and 2022, its recommendations yielded an annualized return of 11.8 percent. If a subscriber had invested $1,000 in 1986, and continued following its recommendations until 2022, they would have ended up with $55,450.43.

After the first decade of positive returns, when the mysterious G. Weiss finally revealed herself on *Wall $treet Week*, many of Weiss's subscribers were shocked. They didn't know they were getting all that valuable insight from a woman. But after getting positive returns for such a long time, many subscribers of the newsletter didn't care about the gender of the person who helped them to make money. The results spoke for themselves.

Build an Investing Habit by Making It Easy

You form a habit by doing something repeatedly. Epictetus said, "Every habit and faculty is maintained and increased by the corresponding actions: the habit of walking by walking, the habit of running by running. . . . Generally then if you would make anything a habit, do it."

Let's say you want to form a habit of walking daily. That means you walk every day, no matter what the weather is or how busy you are. When it rains, you could walk on a treadmill, if you have one, or go to the gym. This is how we form habits, by consistently performing the action. But most investors don't have an investing habit. They want to invest only when the conditions are perfect. As it happens, every few years, the conditions do seem to be perfect for investing: stock prices go up, interest rates are low, and no recession appears to be looming.

If you want to invest only during those perfect conditions, it's the same as saying, *I will only go for a walk when it's eighty-five degrees without a cloud in the sky and no wind.* If you live on the East Coast, you'd probably go for a walk once a year.

The problem is that most investors are not consistent. They might have a great strategy and buy the best stock in the world, but if they buy only once, they won't reap any significant returns. This is why forming an investing habit will help you to build more wealth.

What's the best way to form a habit? By making the action so simple that it's almost impossible to not do it. We turn to Musonius Rufus for inspiration about habit formation. Out of all the Stoic philosophers, he was the strictest about his habits. That's remarkable because Musonius's father, Capito, was a rich Roman eques (also known as a knight, an honorary title). In the class-based system of ancient Rome, members of the equestrian order were ranked just below senators, which was the highest rank below the emperor.

But instead of pursuing a career in politics (which was a sure way of earning a lot of wealth and power in ancient Rome), Musonius spent most of his life teaching philosophy.

Musonius emphasized the importance of repetition, which is the most important thing when it comes to habit formation. He wrote, "How then would knowing the theory of a thing be better than practicing that theory and doing things in accordance with its guidelines? Although understanding the theory behind the action enables one to speak, it is practice that enables one to act."

The same is true for building wealth. Theory is important, but it's the act, or rather the habit of action, that ensures that you build wealth. I've identified two Stoic laws of consistency that will help you to form an investing habit.

LAW 1: START SMALL

When Geraldine Weiss started investing, she didn't go on a fundraising tour. She didn't ask everyone she knew for money. She started with a small sum of her family's money. Most people assume that you can get rich only by investing big lumps of money. "It takes money to make money," the popular saying goes. But people interpret that to mean "It takes a *lot* of money to make money." That's not true. The whole point of investing is to turn a bit of money into a lot of money. Investing is not a goal, activity, or task; it's a habit. It's something you do regularly, just as you work out, meditate, read, or anything else that takes time to yield results.

If you're just starting out, you can get a feel for investing by adding $50 a month to an S&P 500 index fund. Most brokers allow you to add a dollar amount instead of purchasing a single share (which depends on the quoted price at any given moment). Even if you make plenty of money and live frugally, it's smart to start with small sums to get used to the fluctuations of the stock market.

If you're an experienced stock picker or trader, you can start small after you take a period off or don't perform well. When you come back, invest with small sums. Put on smaller positions and get a few small wins.

This is the same approach that Epictetus proposed to his new students. He didn't think you should start living like a Stoic from day one but rather "start with small things." He gave an example of how you can practice the concept of Stoic indifference: "Suppose you like a ceramic cup you own. Then, if it breaks, you won't be disturbed because ceramic materials tend to break at some point. Then try this with something that you consider a little more precious. Eventually extend this understanding to everything."

When I started practicing Stoicism, I took that approach and applied it to small things and then gradually built it up toward the bigger things in life. Whenever something disturbed me, I would remind myself, *So what? It's just a [fill in the blank]*.

For instance, when my favorite shirt got damaged, I told myself, *It's just a shirt*. When my new dinner table got damaged two weeks after I bought it, I said, *It's just a table*. When I got in a fender bender, I reminded myself, *It's just a car*. And when I injured my foot, I thought, *It's just my foot*.

Even during more significant events, such as getting sick on a trip to Barcelona, I said, *It's just a trip*. Finally, when the S&P 500 declined 15 percent in the fourth quarter of 2018 because of fear of tightening monetary policy, a slowing economy, and an intensifying trade war between the U.S. and China, I reminded myself, *It's just a short-term decline*.

I never could've said that last thing (and meant it) without having started with the first one. Starting small is always the best long-term strategy, because it takes time to form a habit or get used to having a new perspective. One of the reasons I stopped investing in 2008 was because I didn't start small. The prior year, I had taken almost all my savings and bought stocks. No matter how much conviction you have in an investing strategy (even the one I propose in this book), if you go all in from the beginning, you'll only set yourself up for failure. The better approach is to start investing with small sums, see how you respond when your portfolio goes up and down, and train yourself to be patient. Keep adding to your portfolio, slowly but steadily, as you get on with life.

LAW 2: MAKE IT AUTOMATIC

By removing manual decisions from your life, you guarantee that certain actions will be performed. When Geraldine Weiss decided to start *Investment Quality Trends*, she committed to publishing twice per month. The newsletter still continues that publishing schedule today. It's the type of decision that removes a thousand other decisions. By committing to publishing two newsletters a month, she removed human judgment from the equation. No matter what was going on in the market or her personal life, Weiss kept publishing new issues of *Investment Quality Trends*.

How many projects have you started with passion and excitement, only to quit after a short while? Inconsistency nearly always results in failure. It's easy to be inconsistent. We have responsibilities, jobs, people to take care of, and so forth. There is always something that stands in the way of achieving your goals. So give yourself no option but to be consistent. When I started my weekly newsletter in 2015, I committed to publishing two editions a week for as long as I could. I kept up that pace for nearly three years. In that time, my newsletter grew from zero subscribers to more than fifty thousand. I've since changed my publishing schedule, but I still honor that commitment to publish every single week. Without sticking to a set schedule, I wouldn't have any reason to write every week. But by publicly committing to a publishing schedule, I made my writing automatic. No matter how tired or busy I was, the newsletter had to happen.

When you want to invest in the stock market, your own emotions and judgments are often your biggest enemy. When the market is going up and interest rates are low, you're likely to take on more risk than you can handle. When things are bad, you're likely to avoid all risk. Automating your finances removes your emotions from the equation. That can be as simple as setting up rules like this for yourself:

- I'm investing $500 a month in my S&P 500 index fund. (You can set that up to happen automatically inside your 401(k), IRA, or pension account.)
- I'm not going to buy any new clothes, tools, or other desirable items for six months.

The key is to stick to these rules always—not just during good times. When you decide to invest a certain amount every month, avoid changing the amount when the stock market goes up or down. You can make changes based on your own circumstances; when you earn more, invest more. But avoid making changes based on what the market does. Look at your own situation and decide how much money you can invest. My motto is "Invest as much as you won't *miss* every month." Avoid picking a number that makes it impossible for you to cover your cost of living. I discuss the details of how much to invest and how to invest in the Stoic Investing Techniques section.

Most people assume that automating your finances means using budgeting apps, measuring every incoming and outgoing cent, and staying on top of your money every day. But this is not a Stoic approach. The idea behind Stoicism is to do everything you do for one reason: to optimize for tranquility and happiness in your life.

Musonius put it best: "For there is no other reason for becoming good than to be happy and live a blessed life thereafter." Similarly, there's no other reason for saving and investing than to be happy and free. The moment you notice that any of your personal-finance behaviors stands in the way of true

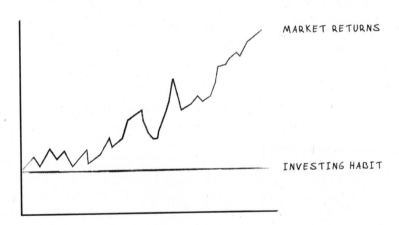

Figure 7: A habit is consistent; the market is not. When you focus on what you control (your behavior), you ensure that you keep investing regardless of what's going on in the market.

happiness, it's time to rethink that activity. You want to make saving and investing automatic. Only simple things can be automatic.

MEDITATE ON THIS . . .

It does not make much difference whether you abandon philosophy or interrupt it, since it does not persist when it is interrupted but, like things which burst when inflated, slips right back to where it started, because it has lost its continuity.

—Seneca

Once you abandon investing, it's hard to come back to it. As Seneca says, without consistency, we will fall back on our old routines.

This is why you must prioritize consistency over everything else. When you start investing, think about how you can set yourself up for long-term success. As a Stoic, your first question shouldn't be *How can I generate the highest return?*

It should be *How can I ensure I'm consistent with my investments?* You will build more wealth if you consistently invest small sums than if you occasionally invest big sums.

· CHAPTER SUMMARY ·

- Investing is a habit, not a one-time task or activity. Start viewing investing like any other habit you live by. When you turn investing into a recurring activity, you can effortlessly start building true wealth.

- As with any habit, consistency is key. Decide to be a consistent investor and pick a strategy that you can consistently stick to.
- Start investing with small sums. When you start investing, the most sustainable strategy is to start small. Even if you've saved up a large amount of money, still start small and get used to the ups and downs of the market.
- Pick an amount you can invest every single month. As a Stoic investor, focus on the most important thing you control, which is how much you invest. Because you don't control what the market does, it's a waste of energy to pay attention to it.

Accept Loss

If you want to improve, be content to be thought foolish and stupid with regard to external things.

—EPICTETUS

· 7 ·

Get Comfortable with Short-Term Losses

t's natural to fear loss. The thought of losing money is so painful that most people never even start investing. However, both Stoics and successful investors perceive loss differently, viewing it as a temporary and inevitable aspect of the process. By adopting this mindset and becoming comfortable with the occasional short-term loss, you can ensure long-term success by staying committed to your investment strategy. This shift in perspective on money and life will bolster your confidence in the future, as you recognize that certain losses are merely transient and an integral part of your wealth-building journey.

Betting on a Prosperous Future

Born in 1955 to Irish immigrant parents in the United States, Cathie Wood grew up in an environment that forced her and her family to build their life from scratch. "I was very fearful as I went into college," Wood remembered. "I was the oldest and I had to carry the mantle for the family. And so I approached it with a great bit of trepidation." That type of anxiety is not uncommon for first-generation immigrants, and the uncertainty of the 1970s made it worse.

It was a time of high inflation and high unemployment. Wood's family struggled financially. Throughout college, she worked at supermarkets and restaurants so she could pay her own tuition. "I thought I'd go into geology, astronomy, engineering," she recalled, before her father nudged her toward economics. Wood eventually decided that studying economics would give her better prospects for financial security.

While she was studying at the University of Southern California, Wood's interest in economics was sparked by her economics professor Art Laffer, who mentored her and encouraged her to take graduate-level classes. In 1977, while she was in her junior year, Laffer helped her secure an internship at Capital Group, a firm with a reputation for long-term vision and research. It was during her first assignment, which required her to think about what Hong Kong would look like twenty years in the future, that Wood had a "wow moment." Her perspective on the world changed. "The focus on such a long-term time horizon was one of the things that really got me. I said, 'OK, this is what I want to do.'"

Wood went from intern to assistant economist at Capital Group, working full time while also studying at USC. In 1981, she graduated summa cum laude with a bachelor of science degree in finance and economics.

Wood then moved to Jennison Associates to be an asset manager in New York. Over the course of her eighteen-year tenure, she became chief economist and managing director. After two decades climbing the corporate ladder, she decided to start her own fund. In 1998, she and a former Jennison Associates colleague, Lulu Wang, cofounded the hedge fund Tupelo Capital. This was right in the middle of the dot-com boom of the late nineties, a period when the stocks of internet companies grew exponentially. As the public became more aware of the World Wide Web, investors got more excited about internet stocks. This eventually led to a market bubble and subsequent crash in 2000.

The crash affected nearly all growth investors and money managers, including Tupelo Capital. Tupelo had roughly $1.3 billion in total assets under management (AUM) in the first quarter of 2000, according to its Securities and Exchange Commission filings. By early 2001, Tupelo's total AUM had fallen to around $200 million. That's an 85 percent loss. That same year, Wood decided to leave her own fund and join AllianceBernstein, a global asset management firm.

Wood managed various types of funds at work, but she was most passionate about disruptive and innovative technology companies. But she realized that she was limited in her ability to invest in projects with true long-term horizons. Major asset managers like AllianceBernstein have two objectives. They act as fiduciaries for their clients, meaning they have a legal and ethical obligation to act in the best interest of their clients. But at the same time, asset managers are for-profit organizations with the goal of growing their revenue. This dynamic generally creates a short-term bias, which didn't align with Wood's philosophy.

In 2012, she came up with the idea of investing in disruptive tech companies through ETFs that would be widely available to the public. Investing in disruptive technology generally doesn't lead to short-term (one-to-two-year) returns. Wood proposed to invest in companies that had the potential to give positive returns within a five-year time frame. She pitched her idea to the executives at AllianceBernstein, but in line with expectations, they passed on her idea.

Two years later, Wood decided to pursue the strategy she had proposed on her own. In 2014, she started her investment management firm, ARK Invest. Her firm focused on investing in new companies in groundbreaking fields like artificial intelligence, gene editing, robotics, and cryptocurrencies. Many traditional money managers avoid start-ups and new industries because they are more likely to fail. According to an analysis by Nasdaq, which is well known for its technology listings, 80 percent of companies that go public never become profitable.

When Wood started ARK, she published its trades every day on its website and via an email blast to subscribers. This transparency is in stark contrast to major hedge funds, which are obliged to publish their holdings only at every end of the quarter with the SEC. With this strategy, Wood pursues the goal that many of the companies she invests in have, which is to improve transparency in traditional industries.

Hedge funds avoid transparency because they don't want competitors to front-run or "short" their stock picks. It's something many other investors also do. They fear that their investing strategy might stop working if others latch on. But ARK takes the opposite approach: the more people know about something, the better.

As Wood expected, her strategy didn't work instantly. In 2016, two years after she founded ARK Invest, Wood posted negative annual returns with her main fund (the Innovation ETF, ticker symbol ARKK). The fund was down 2 percent that year. In comparison, the S&P 500 was up 12 percent in 2016. The difference in performance was 14 percentage points, a large margin.

Things were so bad that Wood approached various companies to attract more capital, because it seemed like no one trusted her with their money. She even signed an agreement that provided an option for her distributor to buy controlling shares—which placed Wood's ownership in a dangerous position. If the distributor company chose to buy her out, she'd risk a hostile takeover of the company she had built. But she took that risk to raise the capital she needed. By the end of 2016, Wood had sunk over $5 million of her own money into the fund to keep the business going. Despite the underperformance of the ARK fund so far, Wood believed she was on the right track.

The following year, in 2017, ARK's main fund went up by more than 87 percent. The fund had a 3.5 percent return in 2018, but it regained its momentum the following year, finishing 2019 with a 35 percent return.

But Cathie Wood's biggest breakthrough came in 2020, when she accomplished a record gain of over 152 percent. For comparison, the S&P 500 posted a "meager" 18 percent gain in the same year. Cathie Wood outperformed the market massively, and she finally received widespread praise from the media. The fund had grown from a few million dollars in 2016 to $3.6 billion in 2020. Boosted by a major presence in the media, ARK kept growing in size and popularity. By early 2021, ARK had $50 billion in AUM. Despite the subsequent bear market that started in 2022, when the market fell more than 20 percent, Wood no longer had to knock on people's doors for money. Instead, investors kept coming to her.

As tech companies experienced a downtrend in 2022, Wood's critics began predicting her fund's demise. But though her main fund was down 67 percent that year, Wood continued to stick to her strategy. In a December 2022 tweet, she told her followers that ARK was "sacrificing short-term profitability for exponential and highly profitable long-term growth." Ever since her college internship, Wood has had a long-term perspective on investing. The wild swings of the market haven't made an impact on her strategy.

Three Steps to Becoming Better at Dealing with Financial Loss

Throughout Cathie Wood's career, she has shown a passion for innovative companies. Her big bet on Tesla is the perfect example of this. In 2018, Tesla's stock price was getting hammered and the company was just a month away from bankruptcy.

Tesla traded at around $22 per share. But Wood boldly stated that these shares would surge to around $260 in five years. She predicted a massive 1,200 percent increase in upside potential. A year later, Tesla stock was down 41 percent, which caused many people to doubt her prediction. But in January 2021, two years earlier than Wood's prediction, Tesla's shares hit $408, an increase of 1,900 percent.

Every time one of Wood's funds or favorite stocks is down, the media highlights how much ARK is down and questions her investment thesis. But Wood has learned not to let short-term loss—or public doubt—affect her long-term strategy.

When most of us face a loss in the stock market, we naturally tend to proceed with caution. *I don't want that to happen again.* We behave like a child who touches fire for the first time and learns to be cautious to avoid pain. But we need to overcome our natural tendency toward avoidance if we want to build long-term wealth.

You don't need to make moves as extreme as Wood's, but you do need to get comfortable with ups and downs. Every year, the stock market typically experiences multiple "pullbacks" or "corrections," which are defined as a decline of 5 percent to 10 percent and between 10 percent and 20 percent respectively. As a Stoic, you must be comfortable with this type of loss. It's natural. And we need to learn to accept what's natural. We don't think these natural fluctuations are good or bad; we simply see them for what they are—short-term losses.

The worst thing you can do is to let losses of the past influence your decision-making. It's good to protect your money and to avoid preventable mistakes. However, it's not in your best interest to be so afraid to lose that you stop investing. This is particularly true for investing in the S&P 500, which has never underperformed over the long term. You make your losses permanent only when you sell too soon.

To overcome the discomfort of short-term losses, it's essential to develop the skill of embracing temporary setbacks. It simply requires self-awareness and creating mental cues that help you to stay Stoic when you have the urge to do something irrational. The following three steps will help you in building resilience and becoming more at ease with losses.

1. NEVER LET THEM SEE YOU SWEAT.

In *Meditations*, Marcus Aurelius talked about the lessons he learned from the people he looked up to in life. One of those people was his adoptive father, Antoninus Pius, who is mostly known for being one of the "Five Good Emperors" of the Roman Empire during the second century AD. During his eighty-four-year reign, he never deployed the military and he protected peace.

About his adoptive father Marcus wrote the following: "He never exhibited rudeness, lost control of himself, or turned violent. No one ever saw him sweat. Everything was to be approached logically and with due consideration, in a calm and orderly fashion but decisively, and with no loose ends." This is a great standard to live up to for every one of us. Like Antoninus Pius, we must strive to be calm and restrained, especially in front of other people. When we set a high bar for our behavior in front of others, we tend to live up to it more. This is a peculiar trait of humans. We often behave differently in front of strangers or acquaintances compared with when we're alone or with family. While we're more restrained in public, we can be irrational in private. But to the Stoics, this was not the right way to live. They believed you should be the same person in every single situation in life.

Think about it. We often brush off minor inconveniences in front of others. When we're at work, we're more tolerant of other people's behavior. When your coworker spills coffee on the table, you say, "No problem!" But when your partner does it at home, you might roll your eyes or make a snarky comment. The Stoics aimed for consistent behavior. If you tell your coworker it's not a problem when they spill something, you need to tell the same thing to your partner or family member. When you extrapolate this behavior, you can start practicing calm by never letting other people see you sweat about small things.

The next time the market is down, imagine someone asking you, *So, how do you feel about this bear market? How much money have you lost?* Go over that conversation in your mind or in your journal. Imagine saying something like *I think I'm down a few thousand dollars. But it's temporary. The S&P 500 has always recovered. I'm not in risky assets. There's nothing to worry about. What else is new?*

Brush it off. Treat it like a minor thing. It's normal to think, *If I sell and get out now, at least I won't feel that bad anymore.* But that's not the answer. Consider what Cathie Wood does.

If you watch an interview with her during a stock market correction, you see a serene investor at the top of her game who doesn't have a care in the world. But let's face it, on the inside, she probably feels just as bad as any other person who's losing money. It doesn't matter if you're down $100 and Cathie Wood is down $1 billion. You both feel the loss in your gut.

But when you go on the record saying that everything is okay, you start believing your own story. If you keep rationalizing short-term declines in the S&P 500 like that, you eventually get more comfortable with the fluctuations in your portfolio.

2. DO NOTHING WHEN THE MARKET CRASHES.

In one of his correspondences with his friend Lucilius, Seneca talked about how his baker sold out of bread one day. Seneca simply showed up too late. "My baker has no bread, but the bailiff has some, and the doorman, and the tenant. 'Bad bread!' you will say." Seneca talked about how the people who did get bread were quick to complain. They didn't appreciate their bread because they were not hungry. "Wait, and it will become good; hunger will make even this soft and refined, so you should not eat before hunger orders it. So I shall wait and not eat until I either begin to have good bread or stop turning up my nose at bad bread. One must get used to a little; many difficulties of place and time arise even for men well off and well equipped to prevent and obstruct the man wanting something."

In the history of the S&P 500, the index has closed in the green between 50 percent and 60 percent of the days when stocks traded. That means it's more likely your portfolio will be up when you open your stock account on any given day. And because the stock market is up most days of the year, that's what we get used to, especially in a bull market.

As Seneca told his friend, one must also get used to a little difficulty. If life is easy, we get frustrated quickly. When you're sated, you're not in the mood to have so-so bread. But if you haven't eaten in more than a day and you're hungry, that same loaf of bread tastes amazing.

It's the same with your investments. When you see your

portfolio going up over a long period, you can't stand seeing it going down. But what would you do if you had no money? You would take any money. Just as Seneca reminds his friends that everything in life is about perspective, we can also remind ourselves that losing money with a long-term investing strategy is not bad. You're not broke. You still have your income, and your stock portfolio is not wiped out. Sure, it might be less than yesterday, but you're not starving either. This is the key to staying calm when the market starts going down.

During market panics like 2008 or the COVID-19 crash of 2020, there are the days you get notifications like "BREAK-ING: Dow sinks 3,000 points in worst day since 1929." Even the most poised investor gets scared reading those types of fear-inducing headlines. The last thing you want to do, though, is something stupid. You might get the urge to sell because there's so much negativity. But a Stoic investor realizes it's nothing to worry about.

It makes no sense to change your strategy when there's a global event that takes down your portfolio. And those types of events will happen multiple times. It's not a matter of "if." You will experience several major crashes during your lifetime. These crashes especially hurt when you've been investing for thirty years and you've built substantial wealth. What will you do when you're down $300,000 in a day? Nothing.

Like the Stoics, you always need to put things in perspective. When you do that, your fear will go away. None of this should impact your strategy. You are not in the business of predicting what markets do.

When the next crash happens, remember Seneca. We're not used to setbacks. We're used to seeing a stock market that goes up most of the time. You're not broke, and you certainly don't rely on your investments to pay the bills. Simply sit it out.

3. INVEST MORE IF YOU CAN.

Imagine that the stock market has gone down for three months. Your portfolio is down 15 percent on the year, but you're calm. At the same time, you also recognize that the market is lower than it was three months ago. If your favorite toothpaste is on sale, you buy more of it to save money. The same is true in the stock market, if you're a long-term investor. When assets are on sale, you can get in at a lower price.

But here's the catch: buy only when you *can*. You probably don't borrow money to buy your toothpaste just because it's on sale. You simply wait until next month and buy it at the normal price.

When a stock that Cathie Wood owns goes down for no apparent reason, which often happens to growth stocks, she buys more if she has extra cash. For example, in early 2023, when Tesla and Coinbase were down, she made $42 million and $22 million purchases, respectively. But those stocks were also down the prior year. She didn't buy more on every single pullback, only when she had extra cash and saw an opportunity to buy her favorite stocks at lower prices.

When the S&P 500 is down more than 10 percent, it's an opportunity to use cash to invest more if you have the financial flexibility to do so. Apply the same strategy during a bear market (when the market declines more than 20 percent), which happens roughly once every four years.

If you're a stock picker, you must proceed with more caution. You want to avoid a "falling knife," which is a stock that's rapidly tanking with no clear signs of recovery. You will see a lot of growth stocks (which are not part of the S&P 500 index) get caught in a downward spiral. Buying stocks that are going down fast is not a good strategy.

If you have an appetite for risk and picking stocks, at least use the "90/10 rule of speculation." This is a strategy I created for minimizing losses. You can read more about it in chapter 15. The idea is to invest 90 percent of your capital in a broad index like the S&P 500. Allocate 10 percent of your capital to more speculative investments. That way you will be less affected when your stock picks don't work out.

Whether you're a passive investor or a stock picker, simply remember to invest more when the market is down if you have the opportunity. How much more? If you want to build wealth faster, as much as you can.

Let's say you usually invest on the first day of every month, and by the twentieth day of the month, the market is down 16 percent. You're thinking about buying a new TV with the money in your checking account, but you see that the market is giving you an opportunity to compound your money. If you are deciding between buying a consumer product and taking advantage of a market pullback, always choose the latter. That product you want but don't need can wait. The market doesn't.

> **MEDITATE ON THIS . . .**
>
> *The soul is strengthened as it is trained for courage by enduring hardships and trained for self-control by abstaining from pleasures.*
> —Musonius Rufus

Imagine you have a substantial amount of money in the stock market. Your portfolio was worth $350,000 just four days ago. Since then, the market has dropped on the threat of a recession. The first day, it went down 4 percent, the second day it was 2 percent lower, then it dropped 1.5 percent, and finally another 5 percent down.

A 12.5 percent drop in less than a week has happened before in history. Your portfolio is now worth $306,250. You lost nearly $50,000 in four trading days. Think of how your stomach feels when you lose that amount of money. For many of us, it's a year's salary. Regularly meditate on these types of losses—especially during bull markets. Analyze how you would react and how bad you might feel; anticipating the worst takes the sting out of it. Doing these mental exercises prepares you for when real loss comes.

• CHAPTER SUMMARY •

- The fear of loss is normal. But listening to that fear and *not* investing will keep you from building wealth.
- Acquiring the capability to be comfortable with losses will make you wealthier. When you keep investing through losses, you make sure you stay invested. Simply by the act of continuing, you guarantee your profit from the market's long-term upward motion.
- Our lives and careers are long, and loss is inevitable. Trying to avoid loss is fruitless. You're better off working and investing through it.
- When you experience temporary setbacks, never let them see you sweat. Keep your cool in front of others, and it will eventually become a part of your character.
- Never give in to the pressure to act on day one of a market crash. Just observe and see what happens. In

most cases, the market rebounds within a few days. If it doesn't, consider investing more.

- When the market is down more than 10 percent, invest more if you can. If you have spare cash, invest it in the market instead of letting it sit in your savings account.

· 8 ·

Avoid Losing All Your Money

As your wealth begins to increase, the temptation to take on more risk for the sake of higher returns can be alluring. However, an excessive focus on potential gains often leads to permanent losses and, ultimately, financial ruin. To safeguard your growing wealth and promote continued growth, it's vital to steer clear of significant losses that you can't come back from. By being aware of the most prevalent causes of financial downfall, you'll be better equipped to avoid unnecessary risks, recognizing that the potential consequences far outweigh the potential rewards. The key to sustained growth lies in preventing losses.

The Gambling Math Professor Who Couldn't Lose

Everyone who has ever visited a casino knows that the house always wins. That's why most people don't go to Las Vegas to make money but to have a good time. But the mathematician Edward Thorp saw casinos as a place he could make a living.

Thorp, born in 1932, received his PhD in mathematics from the University of California, Los Angeles, in 1958. He went on to work until 1961 at MIT, where he directly worked with Claude Shannon, the "father of information theory." Shannon's mathematics theories laid the groundwork for the electronic communications networks that cover the entire planet today.

It's no wonder Thorp looked at everything as a mathematical equation. From his point of view, the game of blackjack, also called twenty-one, wasn't a pure game of luck: it was math that you could beat.

When he boldly shared his opinion in a peer-reviewed journal article called "A Favorable Strategy for 21" in 1961, national papers quickly picked up the story. Naturally, casino owners and employees didn't believe him. Thorp remembers a casino spokesman who ridiculed his system on television. "When a lamb goes to the slaughter, the lamb might kill the butcher. But we always bet on the butcher," the spokesman said.

When a wealthy gambler heard about Thorp's claim, he offered him $10,000 to visit Reno and beat the casinos, in hopes of learning a trick or two. Thorp pocketed $11,000 on that trip after repaying the $10,000, more than doubling the money he had started with.

He perfected his system and published a book in 1966 called *Beat the Dealer*, which documented his strategy for winning at blackjack without cheating. The book became a major success and caused a "blackjack craze" across America. People loved the fact that Thorp put his theory into practice and actually made money. The experience taught him an important lesson: if you have an edge in a certain game, you can win if you play long enough.

If he did lose a hand, he would lose only a small amount relative to his wins. He didn't get wiped out like many other casino players who didn't take it seriously, were drinking, and allowed their emotions to get to them. When the probabilities were on his side, he would bet big, and if they weren't, he bet small. His aim was to go home with more than a year's salary's worth of winnings in his pocket.

"This plan, of betting only at a level at which I was emotionally comfortable and not advancing until I was ready, enabled me to play my system with a calm and disciplined accuracy," Thorp reflected.

After Thorp published *Beat the Dealer,* and more people learned to count cards, the casinos changed the rules and introduced multideck blackjack. This neutralized Thorp's system of counting cards. Over time, casinos started cracking down on card counters.

Thorp knew his blackjack days were over. He left Vegas for Wall Street, which he called the "greatest gambling arena on earth." He wanted to do for stocks what he had done for twenty-one. In 1969, Thorp quit his academic career and collaborated with securities traders to form a hedge fund called Princeton Newport Partners.

The first stock Thorp bought was a company called Electric Autolite, which produced automobile batteries for Ford Motors, among others. He found positive reviews of Electric Autolite in the news, so he decided to use some of his blackjack winnings and book sales to buy shares. He bought a hundred shares at $40 a share and watched the stock decline to $20 over two years.

Thorp lost half of his $4,000 investment. Like a gambler who's down, he insisted on playing until he got even, and hung on to the stock until it returned to its original price. It took four years for Electric Autolite's stock to climb back to Thorp's original purchase price. During that time, the S&P 500 posted better returns, which made him realize he wasn't winning at all. Thorp simply recouped his money in four years, while the index posted a 16 percent gain during the same period (1969–73).

He asked his wife, Vivian, "What were my mistakes?" Thorp often consulted his wife on his endeavors. Vivian bluntly told him that he was playing a game he didn't understand. She was right. Thorp was out of his element on Wall Street. He reflected on some of the lessons he learned during his time playing blackjack: (1) understand the game you're playing; (2) stay in the game long enough to bet big when the probabilities are on your side; and (3) expect loss. He wasn't living by those rules when he started investing. Thorp adjusted his strategy and started to invest by his rules more strictly.

By 1975, six years after he started investing, Thorp had become a millionaire. As Thorp's name grew in the investing world, he met more people in the industry. He observed that there were people who "seemed to be lacking a moral compass." He remembers introducing one of these characters to Vivian one day. Later, after the meeting, Vivian said he shouldn't trust the guy. Thorp asked why. "You can see he's greedy from the way he drives," Vivian replied.

Despite being one of the first Wall Street "quants," or investors who rely on math to make their decisions, Thorp understood that the finance business wasn't only about numbers; it was also about whom you associated with. He avoided losing money by avoiding people and companies he didn't trust. In 1994, a famous trader named John Meriwether, together with two future (1997) winners of the Nobel Prize in Economic Sciences, founded a hedge fund called Long-Term Capital Management. The fund boasted sixteen general partners who were distinguished academics and veteran traders. They even included a former Federal Reserve vice chairman. The fund's investors also included nearly all the major American investment banks. That might have not been unusual for a hedge fund. However, LTCM also secured funding from the central banks of Italy, Singapore, Taiwan, and Thailand. These entities generally do not invest in hedge funds.

One day, people from LTCM approached Thorp and asked if was interested in investing in the fund. At the time, LTCM was the most popular fund on Wall Street because of its exceptional returns. It achieved returns (after fees) of 21 percent in its first year, 43 percent in its second year, and 41 percent in the third year. But Thorp did a little digging and didn't think the returns were sustainable. He also didn't trust the character of Meriwether, one of the fund's leading partners. "Meriwether had a history at Salomon of being a major risk taker," Thorp reflected. "The partnership's theorists were, I believed, lacking in 'street smarts' and practical investment experience." Thorp declined.

In 1998, just four years after it was founded, Long-Term Capital Management's investments plummeted. The fund lost almost 90 percent of its capital in a matter of weeks, which caused a major ripple in the global financial industry. But LTCM was "too big to fail," so it was bailed out, a precursor to the financial crisis of 2008.

The Federal Reserve brokered an agreement with other financial institutions so the fund could be liquidated without doing damage to the global markets. One year after the biggest hedge fund failure in history, Meriwether and four other former partners pompously started another hedge fund called JWM Partners.

In 2009, during the aftermath of the financial crisis, that fund also collapsed. In 2010, Meriwether started yet another hedge fund. And the cycle went on. It was a practice that Thorp called "Heads we win, tails you lose." Hedge fund managers typically earn money through management fees, whether they make a profit or not. When a fund underperforms, the manager can simply shut the fund down and start a new one. The investors must swallow the losses. But Thorp's entire strategy revolved around avoiding losses.

Thorp reported that his personal investments had generated a 20 percent average annual return since he started investing, and he never had a losing year. He and Vivian decided they had made enough money to be comfortable for the rest of their lives.

Thorp reflected, "Success on Wall Street was getting the most money. Success for us was having the best life."

Avoid Loss with the Three Stoic Rules for Sound Investing

When you buy and sell risky assets like index futures, stock options, or cryptocurrencies, you experience either a permanent profit or a permanent loss on every trade. This binary outcome is a huge difference from investing. When you invest in assets with underlying value, like stocks of solid companies, permanent loss happens only when you sell prematurely during a crash or the company goes bust. While the former often happens because it comes down to investor behavior, the latter is very unlikely for established and profitable companies.

When LTCM approached Edward Thorp, he didn't look at the potential upside. He looked at the potential loss, which could have been devastating. While it seems like LTCM got wiped out because of one big mistake, the hedge fund made a *series* of mistakes. Just as you can positively compound your money with good returns, you can negatively compound your money. These small losses lead to big wealth destruction. Few investors lose their entire wealth because of one bad investment.

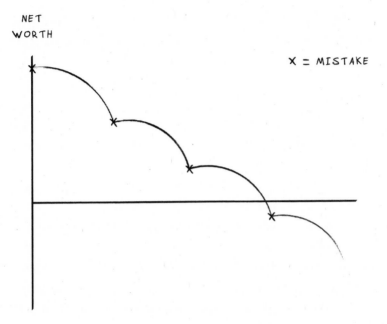

Figure 8: A series of mistakes that lead to losing money build up over time. With every loss, a person's net worth keeps going down, with the possibility of going below zero (a negative net worth).

The majority of investors who destroy their wealth do so after a sequence of bad decisions.

The Roman poet Juvenal, who subscribed to many of the Stoic beliefs, once said: "No one ever suddenly became depraved." People destroy their lives not because of one bad decision but because of a series of bad decisions held up for a longer time.

The emphasis on avoiding mistakes also characterized Edward Thorp's investing career. Everything he did was focused on one thing: avoiding losses. He realized that small losses add up and that at some point you've lost so much you can never come back. What follows are my Three Stoic Rules for Sound

Investing. Subscribing to these rules, which have underlying principles in Stoic thought, will help you to avoid major financial blows.

1. INVEST IN WHAT YOU KNOW.

How do you know what the correct price is for a stock? It's such a complex task that every investing expert and finance professor has a different opinion. This is exactly why investing is more art than science. Ask ten investors what company X is worth, and you'll probably get ten different answers. Because there's no universal way to judge an investment, you have to pick a valuation model. One of the most popular models uses the price-to-earnings (P/E) ratio of a company, which measures the current market value of a company's stock price compared with its earnings per share (EPS). In the simplest terms, a high P/E ratio may indicate that a company is overvalued, while a low P/E ratio may suggest that the company is undervalued. However, the stocks with the highest P/E ratios are generally the ones that go up the fastest, which is why valuation models usually don't say anything about the short-term movement of a stock.

Investors like Edward Thorp are famous for spending countless hours on research to determine what price they should pay for a stock. There are so many factors that determine the value of a stock that it's a topic hundreds of people write books about every year. The idea is that if you learn the skill of valuation, you will make good investments.

But most of us don't have the desire to spend hours every day evaluating stocks. We don't have the passion or interest to read a company's balance sheet and annual report. We don't care about how a company performs in its industry and what its prospects are. We don't know who its CEO is or what their values are. And yet many of us have bought stocks of companies because we use their products or because they were in the news. Many investors call this buying "fashionable" or "glamorous" stocks. Or perhaps we buy a stock from a company that has recently gone public via an IPO. The majority of these newly listed companies underperform the market by a large margin in their first year. Stay away from these types of popular stocks that are often in the news.

Long-term investing is about paying a fair price for a good asset. This is exactly what you do when you invest in the S&P 500. One thing that the investment community agrees on is the efficient-market hypothesis. The idea is that the stock market is always fairly priced because its millions of participants buy underpriced equities and sell overpriced ones. End result? Equilibrium. That doesn't mean the stock market is efficient on a day-to-day basis. In fact, if you look at daily stock charts, you can only conclude that the market is far from efficient when it drops 5 percent because the chair of the Fed said the wrong thing. But in the long term, the stock market is a ruthless self-correcting machine.

Stocks that go up fast usually regress toward the mean. That's the most practical idea behind the efficient-market theory: it's relevant only in the long term. That means you could, in theory, profit from short-term valuation errors. A sophisticated investor who knows the true value of an equity could, in theory, swoop in the moment the price is lower. If you want to buy mispriced stocks, I recommend using the 90/10 rule of speculation (more on that in chapter 15). No matter what your valuation model says, keep in mind that the market might not agree with you.

There's a famous quote attributed to economist John Maynard Keynes: "Markets can remain irrational longer than you can remain solvent." This highlights that markets are always unpredictable, no matter how predictable or rational your arguments are for investing in certain stocks. Even if you're convinced that a stock will eventually turn in your favor, the market can continue to move against you long enough to wipe you out.

We need self-awareness to say, *That's not a game I can or want to play.* The Stoics often talked about the importance of having true self-awareness. In fact, when Marcus Aurelius listed the most important characteristics of a person, he started with self-awareness: "Characteristics of the rational soul: Self-perception, self-examination, and the power to make of itself whatever it wants. It reaps its own harvest, unlike plants."

As Stoic investors we need the self-awareness to recognize that we don't know enough about something to invest in it. When we're enticed to put our money in an individual stock, we must look at ourselves and ask: *Do I know what I'm investing in?* If the answer is no, we must avoid putting our money in those assets.

To invest in the S&P 500, you need to know only about the market as a whole, which is what I explain in this book. You will know how Wall Street operates and what drives the stock market. If you decide to invest in an index fund that mimics the stock market, you're investing in what you know. When you buy something just because it's getting attention or the price is going up, you're not.

2. DON'T INVEST WITH BORROWED MONEY.

Since the founding of the modern stock market in the seventeenth century, we've experienced many booms and busts. It's the nature of a public market. In euphoric moments when the market goes up and up, everyone wants to profit from the seemingly free money in tulips, gold, stocks, real estate, crypto, and on and on. Bubbles are a part of public markets in the same way that injuries are part of sports. You can't have one without the other.

The curious thing is that we all know what causes bubbles. When there's a rush into an asset, people get excited, and they take on more risk than they can handle. Often that means they borrow money to buy an asset. After all, what's the risk of borrowing money to buy stocks that only go up? The common theme of bubbles is that everyone seems to forget financial history. Too much money chasing too few assets always leads to a bubble, which always pops.

In a similar fashion, too much exercise leads to overloading the muscles. When our muscles take on more than they can handle, they experience a breakdown, which comes in the form of an injury. Most injuries come from getting too excited and not knowing our limits. I've been running since I was sixteen. Since then, I've had nearly every injury that's common for runners. And every time I got injured, it was because I taxed my body too much; I've never had an accident type of injury where I fall or roll my ankle. Every time I got injured, I also had to stop running.

The same is true for markets. When too many people borrow too much money, they run up prices. It can take years for this strain to manifest, but eventually the boom cycle comes to an end. Suddenly, prices come crashing down and the market seems to stop suddenly. The people who've borrowed money need to sell their assets to repay their debt. This cycle is destructive to our wealth and our mental health. The reason we take on more than we can handle is because we're impatient. This is something the Stoics wrote about often. We get excited about something, and we want more of it: more money, more pleasure, more exercise, and so forth. But the desire for more, even if you desire something that's good, is not better. Epictetus put it best: "For freedom is not procured by a full enjoyment of what is desired, but by controlling the desire."

Even if we see an opportunity to earn more money, we

must control our desire. Just like the runner who can't build stamina because he's always injured, the investor who borrows money can't build sustainable wealth. The investor who earns a lot during booms also loses a lot during busts. You must avoid this fate as a long-term investor.

But all of this doesn't mean borrowing money is bad. If you're trading stocks for quick profits, borrowing money, or using leverage, can be helpful. Essentially, leverage allows traders to borrow funds to make larger trades than they could with their own capital. While this may seem like a no-brainer, it's important to remember that increased reward comes with increased risk. Using leverage to make larger trades can lead to larger gains, but it can also lead to larger losses. It's important for traders to be ruthless about managing risks. Leverage increases the odds of wiping out your entire trading account. Use leverage only if you make profit on more than 50 percent of your trades and you stick to your strategy like a machine. Never risk more than you can afford to lose.

As long-term investors it's wise for us to avoid leverage altogether. The potential rewards just don't outweigh the risks.

3. INVEST WITH MONEY YOU CAN DO WITHOUT FOR A LONG TIME.

Investing in the stock market is a great long-term strategy. Since 1926, the U.S. stock market has experienced positive returns 95 percent of the time on a ten-year basis. This means that in nearly all ten-year periods during this time frame, investors would have experienced gains in their investments. The only exceptions were the Great Depression and the inflation-ridden 1970s. Other than that, the stock market has been going up steadily.

This means the stock market is a great wealth builder, but we can't count on the market to match its average annual historical return of 10 percent a year in the short term. Just because you're persistently investing doesn't mean you exactly get what you want. As Marcus Aurelius said, we must accept any outcome, "without arrogance, to let it go with indifference." This is especially true in the short run when it comes to investing.

The moment you travel to the future in your mind and say things like *I'm going to use my returns to buy a car next year* or *We can use the stock market returns to pay for our wedding in two years*, you're ignoring the math of long-term investing. That's because you will likely grow your money at roughly 10 percent a year, but only if you give it enough time.

Investing is not a way to generate short-term income. When we invest for the long term, the goal is to put our money to work. But we need to give the money enough time to do the work.

This is why it's critical to invest only the money you won't miss for a decade or more. If you invest with money you need for expenses or large purchases, it's likely you'll be forced to sell your stocks before you allow your money to compound exponentially. What's worse, you might sell at a loss.

While the S&P 500 generated 11.44 percent annual returns on average from 1980 to 2022, any given year might result in negative returns. You can't say things like *My $10K will be $11K next year. That's easy money.* Maybe the market will be down next year. What will you say if that happens? That investing doesn't work and you're only losing money?

To practice Stoicism, you can't be obsessed with when the money will begin to compound. That's because when we're attached to money that we need, we will always be anxious. The most Stoic thing you can do with your money is to say goodbye to it for a long time the moment you invest it in the market. This mental shift will help you to avoid forced selling.

If you need money for unexpected expenses, tap into your emergency fund.

An emergency fund is a separate savings account specifically designated for covering unforeseen costs, such as medical emergencies, car repairs, or job loss. I recommend keeping enough for at least six months' worth of expenses in your fund. I cover this in more depth in chapter 13. By having this financial safety net in place, you can avoid taking on high-interest debt or dipping into your long-term investments when unexpected expenses arise.

If you keep investing with money you might need for expenses or big purchases, you risk getting stuck in a cycle of buying stocks and then engaging in forced selling as soon as you really need that money. As a result, you destroy your potential for building substantial wealth. It's a vicious cycle that keeps you right where you are. You can avoid that by investing only the money you don't immediately need.

MEDITATE ON THIS . . .

A healthy mind should be prepared for anything. The one that keeps saying, "Are my children all right?" or "Everyone must approve of me" is like eyes that can only stand pale colors, or teeth that can handle only mush.

—Marcus Aurelius

Preparation is key, not only in our personal lives but also when it comes to our investing strategy.

Investors can prepare in two ways: (1) by constantly educating themselves on the field of investing; and (2) by learning as much as they can about the particular investment they are making.

When you incorporate those two aspects in your life, you will be prepared for any financial event.

· CHAPTER SUMMARY ·

- Wealth builds faster if you avoid losses rather than focusing on higher returns. As an investor, put more importance on protecting your capital than on optimizing for the potential of higher returns.
- Avoid making common mistakes repeatedly. People destroy their lives not through one bad decision but through a series of bad decisions held up for a longer time.
- Invest in what you know. The S&P 500 index consists of the five hundred best-performing companies in the U.S. It's a simple and understandable investment vehicle. We can't say that for most other financial assets.
- Don't borrow money to invest for the long term. Investing with borrowed money is enticing but puts too much stress on an investor—financially and mentally.
- Invest with money you won't miss. Investing returns are not the same as income. Our careers provide income to live on today; our assets provide returns we can live on in the future.

· 9 ·

Greed Is Not Good

Who doesn't want to be rich and famous? We see other people's extravagant lives filled with luxury, status, and power, and that makes us want the same. We want more of everything: money, opportunities, vacations, food, experiences. But the endless pursuit of more leads to our destruction. When you appreciate that you can have enough of anything in life, you will experience inner peace. You will no longer chase more of everything. You will feel no greed and enjoy what you have.

Getting Ahead by Being Average

It was 1965, the "go-go" era of finance, a time when fund managers who invested in high-risk, high-reward speculative investments were the hottest traders on Wall Street. Investors were leaving conservative, balanced funds in droves to hand over their money to aggressive funds that promised double-digit returns.

One of the traditional firms that was dealing with this exodus was Wellington Management Co. Walter Morgan, the founder of Wellington Management, believed himself to be "too conservative" to continue running the company successfully. When Morgan launched the Wellington Fund in 1929, it was the first balanced fund that invested in relatively safe stocks and bonds. The strategy worked for several decades because the stock market crash of 1929 and the Great Depression that followed made investors, including ordinary Americans, cautious. But the sixties were a different, more prosperous time.

The sixty-six-year-old Morgan called on his then executive vice president, John "Jack" Bogle, and pushed him to "do whatever it takes" to solve the problem. Morgan believed that Wellington had to participate in the go-go tactics of other firms by offering its own speculative funds. The term "go-go" originated in the 1960s, the time when America reached its peak post–World War II growth. The economy and world seemed calm for the first time in decades. Investors took more risk, invested more money, just wanted to go, go, go.

Bogle, born in 1929, didn't have that mentality. He grew up in the tough thirties and forties. He studied economics at Princeton and graduated magna cum laude in 1951. Bogle started working at Wellington right after graduation and worked his way up to a VP position by 1965. Bogle, a risk-averse and pragmatic man driven by his values, nevertheless felt pressure from his boss to participate in the same risk-taking as other firms. With Morgan's approval, Bogle merged Wellington with a go-go firm in 1966. Morgan stepped down later, and Bogle became Wellington's CEO in 1970.

But the market started to show some signs of slowed growth. By 1973, the stock market had started to crash. That year the S&P 500 closed down 17 percent, and it was nearly 30 percent lower the following year. Wellington's assets, which had been valued at $2 billion in 1965, plummeted to $480 million. Bogle was fired in 1974.

Though Bogle had gone along with Morgan's wishes, he never was a proponent of the go-go approach. In fact, in his 1951 Princeton thesis, Bogle had been toying with the idea of creating a fund that yielded less risky returns by tracking the S&P 500. In his mind, the average investor could build more wealth by achieving stable returns over a longer period. He believed it was a fool's game to try to beat the market, exactly the strategy go-go funds followed.

While he always liked the idea of creating an index fund, he never pursued that opportunity until he was fired from Wellington and he read the article "Challenge to Judgement" by MIT economist and Nobel laureate Paul Samuelson. Despite his having just been fired from his job, everything seemed to come together for the forty-five-year-old Bogle.

Why waste your time, money, and energy on picking stocks when you can track the whole stock market through an index and build wealth by simply tagging along? At the time, if you wanted to buy a basket of stocks, you had to either buy every stock separately or invest in an actively managed mutual fund (which came with high costs). This made investing time-consuming, complex, and costly.

That realization inspired Bogle to create a mutual fund that tracked all the companies that were listed on the S&P 500. Because the fund was merely tracking the S&P, it didn't need managers, nor did it have to charge management fees— which significantly lowered costs for investors.

In 1975 Bogle founded his own firm, Vanguard, with the goal of making investing accessible to the average American. In the beginning, the company consisted of Bogle and two employees. Within a year, Vanguard introduced the First Index Investment Trust (now called the Vanguard 500 Index Mutual Fund), a mutual fund that tracked the S&P 500 index.

When Bogle introduced the first index mutual fund, he

was mocked by some people in the investment community. The chairman of Fidelity Investments told the press, "I can't believe that the great mass of investors are going to be satisfied with just receiving average returns. The name of the game is to be the best." People were already calling the mutual fund "Bogle's folly," in anticipation of its downfall. To many people on Wall Street, achieving market returns through passive investing was a "sure path to mediocrity." If one could gain high-double-digit returns in a year, why choose to track the index?

Bogle said that line of thinking was exactly the reason why investment firms had never introduced an index fund. They simply had no motivation to do so. An investment company's objective in forming a mutual fund is to increase assets under management and thus increase advisory fees—which compounds earnings for the firm. The finance industry was built on that system, and no one challenged conventional thinking.

The conventional system was designed to be profitable for investment firms, not necessarily for investors. But Bogle didn't start Vanguard to make money for himself and his firm. He built the firm because he wanted investors to profit from the stock market as a whole. Bogle said, "While all of our peers had the opportunity to create the first index fund, Vanguard alone had the *motivation*."

After Vanguard's rocky start in the midseventies, more people started investing, and they found that Bogle's unique index fund structure was a great match for their financial goals. While Vanguard started with $11 million in AUM, the fund reached $100 million by the end of 1982. Six years later, Vanguard hit the $1 billion fund milestone, ranking 41st among 1,048 funds. More people started investing long term through index funds.

By the end of 2022, Vanguard had $8.1 *trillion* in assets under management, making it the second-largest asset manager in America.

Despite all this wealth creation, Bogle was not a billionaire. When he died at age eighty-nine, in 2019, Bogle was worth $80 million. That's a lot of money by nearly every person's definition. But that's minuscule considering that he pioneered an index fund that's worth trillions of dollars. Meanwhile, the CEO of Fidelity Investments, a competitor that's *half* the asset size of Vanguard, was worth $12.2 billion in the same year.

Bogle regularly gave half of his salary to charity. He often talked about helping other people, and he acted on his words. But more important, he made sure Vanguard didn't profit as much as other investment firms. Bogle believed investment returns must go to the investor. Unlike the typical fund-management companies, Bogle structured Vanguard to be owned not by individual shareholders but by its mutual funds. These funds are owned, in turn, by fund shareholders and are dedicated to low-cost investing. If he and his heirs had been the main shareholders of the company, as was the way most other funds were set up, they would've been multibillionaires for several generations.

Someone once asked the nineteenth-century oil magnate John D. Rockefeller, "How much money is enough money?" And Rockefeller replied, "Just a little bit more." But Jack Bogle didn't agree; he was content to have enough—which was, as he wrote in his book, *Enough*, having "$1 more than you need."

Stoic Exercises for Neutralizing Greed

The entire philosophy of Stoicism is built on the idea of the "golden mean," which is sometimes referred to as the "middle way." From the beginning, the Stoics took a balanced position between two other philosophical movements of the time, namely, Cynicism and Epicureanism.

The Cynics also believed that we become happy when we live in agreement with nature, free from desire for material possessions and social status. But unlike the Stoics, they believed that social constructs (like money) were not a part of living naturally. The Stoics believed we should *adapt* to society. Epicureans, on the other hand, believed that we can achieve happiness by pursuing pleasure while avoiding pain. The Epicureans and Stoics both agreed that we can achieve mental tranquility by living a simple and moderate life. But the Stoics didn't believe in avoiding pain—or anything that's natural, for that matter.

The Stoics chose the middle path. They didn't renounce the pleasures of society, nor did they run away from hardship. They offered a balanced view on every topic in life.

Seneca, one of the wealthier Stoics, talked about the golden mean in relation to money and its excess as follows: "You ask what is the proper measure of wealth? The best measure is to have what is necessary, and next best, to have enough." He agrees with Bogle. We shouldn't renounce wealth like the Cynics, because we need it to live a good life. But we also don't need it in excess so we can fulfill all our desires like the Epicureans.

Balance is easy to define but difficult to achieve. It's in our nature to lean toward excess. In fact, our society emphasizes extremes, and many of us believe it's normal to live on the edge. In finance, you can see that by the amount of credit that's used by investors. When the post-COVID stock market boom started to take off in September 2020, a survey showed that 43 percent of individual investors said they used a form of credit to invest in the stock market.

Using leverage magnifies your potential losses, but it also

magnifies your potential profit. Some investors like the idea of winning it all. However, they don't properly consider the possibility of losing it all. It takes decades to build wealth, but it can get destroyed within a matter of weeks or months.

If you adopt the golden mean, you won't get rich quickly, but you also won't get poor quickly. This trade-off is one that a Stoic would take any day of the week. Living with balance is hard in our modern world, where we're constantly exposed to success stories on social media. We want that for ourselves too. So these stories push us to pursue more of everything.

There is only one way we can ensure we stay balanced: by training ourselves every day. This is one of the most important ideas Musonius Rufus shared in his teachings. He said: "Could someone acquire instant self-control by merely knowing that he must not be conquered by pleasures but without training to resist them?"

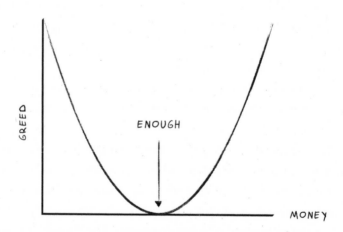

Figure 9: The relationship between greed and money often follows a U curve. When we have little money, we're greedy because we need more to live well. When we have enough money, we can be mentally and practically content with what we have. If we have a lot of money, it's easy to fall into the trap of chasing more for the sake of having more.

In Stoicism, you will find a variety of exercises that inspire you to live better. The idea is that we can never eradicate certain emotions like greed. After all, these are human emotions that happen subconsciously. We can only train our ability to neutralize greed when we feel the emotion. Here are two of the most useful and simplest Stoic exercises to help you adhere to the golden mean.

EXERCISE 1: DESIRE ONLY WHAT'S WITHIN YOUR CONTROL

Epictetus says, "If you desire something outside your control, you are bound to be disappointed." And yet, if you ask any person what they want in life, they nearly always list things that are outside their control:

> "I want to generate 20 percent returns this year."
>
> "When I achieve my income target this quarter, I'll be happy."
>
> "I'm going to work out every day and eat healthy so I can live a long life."
>
> "My goal is to get married by the time I'm thirty, have my first child when I'm thirty-two, and another one when I'm thirty-four."

Every single one of those desires lies outside our control. We can invest in the market, but we can't control the returns. We can try to boost our income, and even if it works, we can still be unhappy. We can work out as much as we want, but we can't control whether we get in an accident or become ill. We can start a relationship, but we can't control our partner's actions or our fertility.

Despite these obvious observations, we insist on desiring things outside our control every day. According to the Stoics, there's nothing wrong with desire, as long as we focus on the things we control. We can desire to improve our knowledge and skills. We can desire to become kinder in the way we treat others. But the moment we desire things that are outside our control, we're opening the gateway to greed. To avoid greed, we must change our self-talk when it comes to those things we don't control. If we can change our language, we eventually change our desires.

> **Go from:** I need/want/wish X to happen.
>
> **To:** It would be nice if X happens.

When I started writing this book, I noticed I would daydream about how the book would become a bestseller and how I would get invited to appear on podcasts and talk shows. I would think, *I want to sell a million copies and have it hit the bestseller list.* Eventually, I adjusted my self-talk. I thought, *What would someone like Seneca think if he wrote a book?*

If it becomes a success, great; if it doesn't, great. We don't control outcomes. We control our effort. I soon started pouring all my energy into writing the best personal investing book in the world. That's my aim. And to me, this is the best book. If others agree, that's great; if they don't, I'm good with that too. Because being liked by others is outside my control, I have no care for it.

Epictetus called this restricting yourself to "choice and refusal." It means that you deliberately choose or refuse every single thing in life over which you have control. You can choose to focus on what you control. You can refuse to get blinded by desire.

EXERCISE 2: MODERATE YOUR HABITS

To live according to the golden mean, we must have self-control. And to train our ability to control ourselves, it's best to start with the most important thing in life: our habits. And according to Musonius, moderation starts with our diet.

Musonius wrote: "The person who eats more than he should makes a mistake. So does the person who eats in a hurry, the person who is enthralled by gourmet food, the person who favors sweets over nutritious foods, and the person who does not share his food equally with his fellow diners." A Stoic should:

1. Never eat more than needed
2. Take enough time to consume food
3. Avoid gourmet food (which is generally pleasurable, calorie dense, luxurious)
4. Avoid sweets
5. Share food with others

If you struggle with self-control, moderating your eating habits is a great way to improve. From there, you can apply moderation to all your habits, which will give you more balance.

I know this from experience. Eating in moderation is something I struggled with in my teens. When I was sixteen and at my heaviest, I weighed 240 pounds. Being overweight bothered me mentally but even more so physically.

When I decided to lose weight, I saw a dietician. She gave me some tips to lose weight, which I can't remember anymore, except for one thing, which I can recount exactly: "Never finish your entire meal as you are trying to lose weight. Always leave just a little bit on your plate. Just a tiny bit, something you think a small animal like a mouse would eat. This is not about limiting your calories. It's about self-control."

Her advice changed the way I ate forever. Within one year, I had lost around fifty pounds through working out six days a week and eating fewer calories than I burned. Once I hit a healthy weight, I always focused on eating enough rather than as much as I could. My weight has been roughly the same for twenty years now.

Every now and then, when I notice I get too greedy with my food, I apply the "leave just a little bit on your plate" technique. It reminds me of the fact that I'm in control of what I eat.

We often underestimate how powerful our self-control is. We assume that our desires are stronger than our self-control. We think it's normal to give in to excess. We can't eat just a handful of chips; we need to eat the whole bag. We can't be satisfied with 10 percent returns in the market; we must have 100 percent.

The way you eat influences the way you live. Indeed, every mealtime or snack offers you a chance to practice. If you're able to eat in moderation, you're also able to live in moderation. Start with what you eat, and the rest of your life will follow.

The underlying principles are the same, whether you apply this thinking to food or to money. When you forget about moderation, you're lost. When you exert self-control, with your diet and with your money, you're in equilibrium. This is what great Stoics and great investors have in common. They are always balanced, whether the market is optimistic or pessimistic. They don't get sucked into the extremes, no matter how big the pull. They are satisfied with having enough.

MEDITATE ON THIS . . .

Is it not madness and the wildest lunacy to desire so much when you can hold so little?

—Seneca

How many clothes do you really wear? How many cars do you need? How many accessories and pieces of furniture can you keep in your house? How many tech gadgets do you use?

The answer to all of the above is often "Not that many." Most of us even prefer living a simple life over the constant pressure to accumulate more.

Meditate on the fact that you get used to everything. Even if you do have many possessions, soon enough, you will get used to everything you own. You can't find lasting pleasure in objects. You can find it only inside yourself.

If you desire anything, desire to live a simple life.

• **CHAPTER SUMMARY** •

- Live by the "golden mean." Avoid excess and aim to live a balanced life. When we live according to the middle way, we avoid financial ruin.
- Focus on building wealth, but not at all costs. The Stoics always chose living according to their values over worldly pursuits like pleasure, status, and money.
- Desire what's within your control. When we want things we can't control, we risk giving up our values

in exchange for what we want. If we don't get what we want, we'll end up frustrated. But if we desire only what we control, we can't be disappointed.

- Moderate your habits. Living a balanced life requires applying moderation to all areas of our lives. When we are good at applying self-control to what we eat, we strengthen our ability to live in moderation.

Compound
Your Money

Moral recommendations behave like seeds. They
achieve a lot, and they occupy little space. Just let the
right kind of mind, as I said, seize on them and absorb
them: then it in turn will produce many ideas from
itself and give back more than it received.

—SENECA

10

Let Your Money Do the Work

When you've acquired some money, you can start turning it into a lot of money. You'll rely on the power of compounding to grow what you have. You will no longer rely solely on exchanging your time for money. This is the true definition of wealth: to break free from the trap of earning money with your time. Instead, you will let your money do the work on its own. Small returns year after year will lead to big results in the long run. When you know that you're consistently investing in the stock market, you know it's only a matter of time before your wealth will grow exponentially. This knowledge will give you satisfaction when you invest.

From Caddy Boy to Managing Billions

Peter Lynch was just ten years old when his father died from cancer in 1954. To help his mother financially, he worked as a caddy at a local country club as a teenager. At the club, Lynch found himself surrounded by continual talk about investing, which opened a whole new world for him. This is where he met George Sullivan, who was the president of Fidelity, one of the largest financial services firms in America. Sullivan and other executives at Fidelity inspired him to try his hand at investing.

During his sophomore year at Boston College, in 1963, Lynch used his savings to buy one hundred shares of Flying Tiger Line at $7 per share. The stock eventually rose to $80 per share; it was a "ten bagger," a term coined by Lynch for stocks that yielded a 10X return. He used his stock market profits to partially pay for the rest of his undergraduate degree, and later even for his graduate degree in business administration at Wharton School. When he was at Wharton, he got an internship at Fidelity Investments because he had been caddying for George Sullivan. That internship turned into a full-time position as an analyst in 1969. He then climbed the corporate ladder and became Fidelity's director of research in 1974.

As Lynch worked his way up, the stock market was going down in 1973 and 1974. In fact, the entire decade was tough for investors; it was dominated by high inflation and an oil crisis, which had a negative impact on markets.

In 1977, sentiment was so bad that brokerage firms closed entire sales departments, because almost no one bought stocks anymore. After his stint as director of research, the thirty-three-year-old Peter Lynch was offered the job of running the Magellan Fund. While Magellan is one of the most famous actively managed mutual funds in the world today, in the 1970s it was small and insignificant, with a mere $18 million in AUM.

As an unproven money manager, Lynch had the opportunity to pick stocks without much pressure. After all, no one expected positive returns in the seventies, especially not from a new manager. But Lynch surprised everyone. Under his leadership, the fund turned things around in 1978. He achieved a 20 percent return, while the Dow Jones Industrial Average, an index of the thirty largest companies in the U.S., lost 17.6 percent and the S&P 500 lost 9.4 percent in the same period.

Lynch's strategy for outperforming the market relied on intensive research. After doing research into a company's books and market, he would often visit the company's shops or offices in person, talking with the people who worked there, learning more about who operated the company. After this exhaustive process Lynch would determine whether it was time to invest in the company or not.

One of the most famous Lynch success stories is his investment in Chrysler. During the seventies, Chrysler's sales were plummeting. The car company had introduced one failed model after another, and financial analysts predicted it would go bust. Based on his research, Lynch decided in 1982 that Chrysler stock was undervalued. The balance sheet showed that Chrysler had more than $1 billion in cash, and Lynch figured investors wrongly assumed the company would go bankrupt, which had sunk the stock price. But before he decided to buy more Chrysler stock, he wanted to meet the management of the company.

In June 1982, Lynch said, he had "probably the most important day in my 21-year investment career." His supposed-to-be-three-hour meeting with Chrysler's execs turned into a seven-hour session. And a "quick chat" with Lee Iacocca, a former Ford executive and Chrysler's CEO, turned into a two-hour session. He also saw the company's latest models on the assembly line. He realized that Chrysler had plenty of new, promising products in the pipeline to sell once the economy recovered.

Cars are cyclical products, which means fewer are sold during economically difficult times and more during prosperous times. But the stock prices of car companies move countercyclically in anticipation of those economic changes. When a car company is posting revenue declines, investors swoop in to buy the stock in anticipation of sales growth. Lynch realized this and started to aggressively buy Chrysler stock. Chrysler was at $2 a share in 1982; it soared to $46 in 1987, making it one of Lynch's most successful stock picks.

The Magellan Fund grew so fast it propelled Lynch to rock-star status in the investing world. He reached his peak celebrity in 1989 when he published the now-classic investing book *One Up on Wall Street.* But running a large fund like Magellan comes with a mental tax. Lynch took his job home during evenings, weekends, and vacations.

Lynch had to track thousands of companies to ensure that the Magellan Fund was investing its resources well. This meant he had to work over ninety hours a week. Lynch remembers going to Ireland—a vacation he was looking forward to, after a long stretch of work—on Thursday, October 15, 1987.

That Monday, October 19, the Dow Jones Industrial Average dropped 22.6 percent of its value. The S&P 500 declined 20.4 percent, which is still the largest one-day drop in the history of the index. To put this drop in perspective, the greatest decline in a single day during the Great Depression was "just" 12 percent.

Instead of enjoying time with his wife abroad, Lynch's mind was terrorized by the latest financial panic. He'd stay up at night, to make up for the time difference, calling his team and instructing them which stocks to dump and which to keep. In the end, he learned two important lessons: (1) don't let nuisances ruin your investments; and (2) don't let nuisances ruin your vacation. Even after the 1987 stock market crash, the market eventually recovered, as always. "Whether it's a 508-point day or a

108-point day, in the end, superior companies will succeed and mediocre companies will fail, and investors in each will be rewarded accordingly," he concluded.

In 1990, Lynch resigned from the Magellan Fund and retired at the age of forty-six. He had grown the fund from $18 million to more than $14 billion in assets with more than one thousand individual stock positions. In an interview on PBS, Lynch was asked why he had retired early. Lynch was one of the top fund managers in U.S. history. Magellan maintained a 29 percent average annual return during Lynch's time, and it had the best twenty-year return of any mutual fund ever.

The interviewer asked Lynch if it was "pressure" that eventually forced him out of the game. Lynch responded: "It wasn't the pressure. I loved the job. I mean I worked for the best company in the world. I got paid extremely well. We had free coffee. . . . The pressure wasn't it. It was just too much time. I was working six days a week and that wasn't even enough."

Lynch compounded his and his investors' money at a fast pace, but his financial results came at a cost: time. He missed out on the defining years of his three young children. After getting excellent returns on his investments for years, Lynch finally realized that he also wanted the same for his time.

Tips for Compounding Money in the Market

If I presented you with the following two options, which one would you choose? Option one: You devote all your free time to obsessing about investing and actively attempting to outperform the market. Let's assume you manage to achieve 2 percent better returns than the market average. However, in exchange for this, you sacrifice all your free time—no time for exercise, no date nights, and no attending your children's recitals. Option two: You adopt a passive investment strategy, allowing your money to grow as the market goes up. You benefit from the power of compounding while enjoying your free time and peace of mind.

Unless you're a finance professional or you're passionate about beating the market, it's likely you chose option two, because it gives you the best of both worlds. You get to build wealth and you can spend your time on the things you truly love.

The good thing about compounding is that it doesn't require you to *do* anything. Simply invest money, achieve a return, then keep investing so you can generate earnings on top of your previously achieved earnings.

When you consistently reinvest your returns and let your money compound, the growth eventually reaches a point where it becomes exponential, resembling the shape of a hockey stick. In the beginning, the progress may seem slow and steady, similar to the straight handle of the hockey stick. However, as the compounding effect takes hold over time, the growth rate accelerates dramatically, like the sharp upward curve of the hockey stick's blade.

While the idea is simple, the execution is one of the hardest things in life. This is because the flat period of the hockey stick generally lasts two decades when it comes to wealth building, and because humans are short-term oriented, we tend to stop investing before we reach the exponential-growth stage of compounding. To avoid that, adopt the mindset of a long-term investor and say to yourself: *I'd rather use my returns when they are big in the future than take out small amounts of money now.*

When you invest and allow your money to compound, you are truly improving your future. The idea of taking time now to prepare for the future is an essential aspect of Stoicism.

Seneca said it best: "Everyone approaches with more courage a hazard for which he has long squared himself, and resists even harsh circumstances by contemplating them in advance. But the man without preparations panics at even the lightest troubles."

To build long-term wealth, we must adopt the same mindset. We face the future with poise because we're investing today. What follows are three tips that will help you to make maximum use of the power of compounding. When you live by these principles, you will let your money grow on its own.

1. OPTIMIZE FOR RETURN ON TIME (ROT).

Peter Lynch was a great investor who shared many wise lessons about investing, money, and business. But his most important lesson was about life: "It was just too much time. I was working six days a week and that wasn't even enough."

Time is not a renewable resource. Once you spend your time, it's gone forever. When you always keep that in mind, you make different decisions, because you think about the return you get. You think: *When I spend my time on this activity, what type of return do I get?* You must ask yourself whether the things you're doing are truly worth it to you. Seneca explained that mindset best: "Let no one rob me of a single day who is not going to make me an adequate return for such a loss."

It's not about being stingy with your time and doing only things that are in your best interest. No, the Stoics simply understood that time must be spent with intention and invested thoughtfully. For Lynch, that meant spending time with his family. Every minute he spent with his family probably gave him more joy and energy than when he spent that on investing. He could make more money spending his time researching companies than spending time with his family. But because he got more value out of family time, he said goodbye to his role as a mutual fund manager.

You can look at this concept as return on time (ROT). When people look at ROI, they look at the financial return of a monetary investment.

- How many cents will you get in return for every dollar you invest? That's ROI.
- How much energy will you get in return for every hour you invest? That's ROT.

Look at the latter first when you make decisions in your life. Look at the alternative to everything that you're doing, and think, *Does the other option give me a better ROT?*

The alternative to active investing is passive investing. Most people look at that trade-off and don't think it's worth it. They look at the low probability of beating the market and the amount of time they have to spend on picking stocks, and go with passive investing because it takes no time.

Albert Einstein called compounding "the eighth wonder of the world" for a reason. Letting your money compound on its own without spending time seems too good to be true, but this is the only exception to the rule.

2. START INVESTING NOW, NOT TOMORROW.

A common theme in Stoicism is this: If you want to do something worthwhile, do it today. If something's not worth doing, don't do it at all. Epictetus once warned his students, "Stop the excuses and the procrastination. This is your life!" He challenged them to take ownership and start living like Stoics right away. We're all inclined to delay important tasks, even if we know it's in our best interest to do them.

To overcome this mindset, you can't rely on tips or hacks. In Epictetus's words, you must "vow to stop disappointing yourself. Separate yourself from the mob. Decide to be extraordinary and do what you need to do—now."

The Stoics challenged us to be exceptional and to fear mediocrity. Living like a sloth was the worst thing that could happen to a Stoic. They understood that living according to Stoic values and being strict with yourself will make you happy.

The same is true of being a disciplined investor. The person who keeps adding to their investments will look back with satisfaction in ten, twenty, and thirty years from now. They will say, *I'm glad I started investing early.* Let that be you.

If you haven't started investing because you're waiting until you earn a certain income, switch careers, pay off a loan, get promoted, are married, and so forth, you're coming up with excuses.

Remember: investing is a habit. It doesn't always matter how much you invest; what matters is that you make it part of your life. That you invest every single month without hesitation. If you're not doing that, start today, not tomorrow. The easiest way is to go to your banking app or online brokerage and buy shares of Vanguard's S&P 500 index (ticker symbol VOO, or VUSA in Europe).

3. AVOID HIGH FEES.

The biggest threats to an investor's long-term returns are costs and fees. The finance industry is just like any other for-profit industry. It must generate profit.

This becomes a problem only when individual investors and traders are not aware of the amount of returns they are giving up because of costs. Some people erroneously assume that financial products and services are free. They assume that buying securities comes with only a one-time transaction cost. But that's not true. Here are the most common costs you must be aware of as an individual investor.

Transaction costs: These are fees you pay to the stockbroker, bank, or intermediary you use to buy securities.

Expense ratios: This refers to the annual fees for an ETF or mutual fund. ETFs generally have fees that are lower than 0.1 percent of total asset value. Actively managed mutual funds have higher costs because they have a staff, so their fees are generally between 0.5 percent and 1.0 percent.

Commissions: If you decide to use a human financial adviser or robo-adviser, you have to take their commissions into account. Financial advisers typically charge 1 percent or more of assets under management per year. Most robo-advisers charge between 0.2 percent and 0.5 percent a year.

Taxes: If you hold your assets in a taxable account (outside your 401(k) or IRA), you might have to pay capital gains taxes. When you buy an ETF as a U.S. taxpayer, you're not charged capital gains taxes unless you sell at a profit. Mutual funds are often structured in a way that means you will probably have to pay capital gains taxes.

The reason I like index funds, particularly Vanguard, is because they are the cheapest way to invest. There's not a fund manager like Peter Lynch, with a staff and an office, whom you need to pay. They charge you a very small fee, often around 1 percent or less. And low-cost index funds often have a fee of less than 0.1 percent, which is one tenth of the fee of a mutual fund.

A few basis points might not sound like much, but when

you give up small amounts of your returns every year, you will leave a lot of money on the table over your lifetime.

Imagine two people: person A and person B. The former buys a Vanguard S&P 500 ETF with an expense ratio of 0.03 percent a year, and the latter buys an actively managed mutual fund with an expense ratio of 0.75 percent.

Let's assume person A and person B each start with $10,000, stick to the same strategy for thirty years, achieve an annualized return of 10 percent, and add $500 a month to their portfolio. Here's what their portfolios look like after thirty years.

- Person A: $1,154,447.96
- Person B: $999,085.61

That's a difference of more than $150,000. The power of compounding leads to big differences because of tiny changes in net returns.

> ### MEDITATE ON THIS . . .
>
> *Given that all must die, it is better to die with distinction than to live long.*
>
> —Musonius Rufus

Imagine yourself on your deathbed. You've invested for a large part of your life, and you sit on a pile of wealth. Think of the satisfaction of leaving that behind in the world.

Think of the lives you can change, way beyond your own lifetime. This is an eternal contribution. In return, you leave with a true sense of peace.

• CHAPTER SUMMARY •

- Let your money compound on its own. Let the power of compounding grow your wealth, and don't look at your investment too often. It takes time before your returns are substantial.

- Prioritize ROT (return on time) over ROI (return on investment). Time is the most important nonrenewable asset in our lives. Focus on getting the most out of your time rather than getting the most out of your money. The potential to earn a few percentage points of returns is often not worth the time.

- Do things that give you energy. Life's too short to obsess about chasing money. Invest. But also do things you truly enjoy.

- Invest today, not tomorrow. We can always think of a reason to not invest, but almost none of them are valid. Form the habit of doing important things right away.

- Avoid high fees. Giving up as little as 1 percent of your returns leads to missing out on large returns over your lifetime. Always keep the costs of investing in mind.

11

Trust Your Judgment

Once you've spent considerable time learning about investing and wealth building, you no longer need to defer to others. You can trust yourself. As the ultimate steward of your own financial well-being, it's crucial to trust your judgment and take full ownership of your responsibilities. Embrace your understanding of investment strategies and have faith in your actions, as they are rooted in logic rather than luck. This mindset empowers you to build wealth with confidence and cultivates long-term financial success.

Breaking Free from "the Greatest Investor That Ever Lived"

Born in 1953 to a middle-class household in Pittsburgh, Pennsylvania, Stanley Druckenmiller graduated from Bowdoin College, in Maine, in 1975 with a BA in English and economics. He briefly pursued a PhD in economics but dropped out to take a job as a securities analyst at Pittsburgh National Bank.

A mere three years later, at the age of twenty-eight, Druckenmiller established his own hedge fund, Duquesne Capital

Management, which quickly found success. Within just three months, one of his funds soared by 40 percent, catapulting the young manager into the limelight as a Wall Street sensation. Eventually, Druckenmiller's success caught the attention of George Soros, founder of the Quantum Fund, which was one of the largest hedge funds, with more than $2 billion AUM in 1987.

After a long and legendary career, the fifty-seven-year-old Soros wanted to focus more on his philanthropic work and take a step back from his fund. Soros had started his own fund in 1969 with $4 million capital, including $250,000 of his own money. Throughout the seventies and early eighties, Soros's reputation grew in the finance community because of the sheer size of his fund. Hedge funds were still relatively small compared with today. A typical fund in the seventies managed tens of millions of dollars. Soros worked with billions. Soros became more famous with the publication of his book *The Alchemy of Finance* in 1987. Druckenmiller had read that book, of course. When Soros reached out to the thirty-five-year-old Druckenmiller and offered him a job at the Quantum Fund in 1988, Druckenmiller was elated but cautious at the same time. Druckenmiller knew that Soros had a reputation for compensating his staff generously but firing them quickly if they didn't perform well. Druckenmiller asked his mentors whether he should take the job or not, and they all advised him not to join Soros.

Why give up his independence at his own fund to join a large fund that was operated by a cutthroat manager? Druckenmiller would give up his freedom. But Soros wanted Druckenmiller on his team badly, so he made him an offer: Druckenmiller could continue to manage his own fund while working for Quantum.

Druckenmiller couldn't refuse. From the start, he was

eager to learn from the experienced Soros, who Druckenmiller called "the greatest investor that ever lived." But this
admiration also came at a price: With Soros's impressive track
record, how could someone like Druckenmiller disagree when
they had different opinions? "Even being coached by the world's
greatest investor is a hindrance rather than a help if he's engaging you actively enough to break your trading rhythm,"
Druckenmiller later reflected.

Soros had trouble letting other people—even his own sup-
posed successor—take over the fund. Druckenmiller ended up
not performing as well as Druckenmiller had expected in his
first year at Quantum. The pressure was mounting and Soros
intimidated him. Though he wasn't a timid person, Druckenmiller couldn't quite keep Soros from second-guessing his decisions. Things came to a head a year later, in August 1989,
when Soros sold a bond position that Druckenmiller really
wanted to keep. And Soros made that decision on his own.

Druckenmiller felt stabbed in the back and yelled at Soros,
"I feel cramped by your presence!" The two had a major argu-
ment, with Druckenmiller concluding, "I want to leave."

This was a turning point for Soros. Did he really want to
keep calling the shots at Quantum? Or would he finally be
willing to give that position to someone else?

"Don't leave," Soros answered. "I'll leave."

With his newly won independence, Druckenmiller began
to take charge without Soros breathing down his neck. By the
end of 1989, Quantum's assets were up 31.5 percent on the
year. The following year, Druckenmiller grew the fund by
29.6 percent, then ramped it up to 53.4 percent by 1991.

Soros was impressed. "It turned out to be a wonderful
move," he reflected after he let Druckenmiller take over. "We
had excellent performance for three years running, another
boom period in the history of the Fund."

The notoriety of the Quantum Fund peaked in 1992, when Druckenmiller helped Soros in a trade that cemented their legacies. During a European currency crisis, Druckenmiller took a massive bet against the British pound. On September 16, 1992—known in Britain as "Black Wednesday"—the British government was forced to exit the European Exchange Rate Mechanism (ERM), which devalued the pound drastically.

As a result, the Quantum Fund's bet generated $1 billion in profits within a single month. Because Soros loved the limelight as much as Druckenmiller wanted to avoid it, the media began attributing the trade mostly to Soros, calling him the man who "broke the Bank of England."

Things were going well until the late nineties, when Soros found it difficult to refrain from intervening, despite his assurances to Druckenmiller. He contacted Druckenmiller, urging him to expand Quantum's investments in technology stocks.

Druckenmiller wasn't confident, calling himself a "dinosaur" when it came to tech. Tech stocks behaved differently from the assets Druckenmiller understood. But he got swayed enough to invest in technology. Pride likely had something to do with it. During the tech boom, Druckenmiller saw how companies that were smaller and had less capital than Quantum multiplied their money tenfold or more. Druckenmiller felt the itch of missing out.

Because he didn't consider himself an expert in tech, he hired a money manager from Silicon Valley, Carson Levit, to support him at Quantum. For the first time, Druckenmiller was outsourcing his judgment to someone else. And it showed in Quantum's bets: unlike Druckenmiller, who bought only assets he thought were reasonably well priced, Levit had no problem paying sky-high prices for inflated tech stocks.

With direction from Levit, Druckenmiller built a portfolio of internet stocks and shorted several blue-chip "old economy" companies like Sears and Goodyear, which they believed would decline as tech companies rose. Their strategy worked. By the end of 1999, the Quantum Fund had a return of 35 percent.

Delighted with their quick profits, Druckenmiller decided to double down on tech. The itch of missing out likely gripped him again. One of Druckenmiller's major bets was a company called Verisign. When the company's stock went up to $258 by late February 2000, Druckenmiller thought that the price would keep going up. He bought $600 million worth of the stock in early March when Verisign's price dropped to $240, which seemed like a short-lived pullback. But a month later the Nasdaq tumbled and Verisign's stock fell to $135, a staggering 44 percent decline from the March price.

The atmosphere at Quantum turned bleak. To relieve stress, traders on the floor started playing with Koosh balls (furry toys that were popular in the early 2000s) and Druckenmiller went more frequently to the gym. But the rest of the time, he slumped in his office and quietly watched the market.

With losses that big, Soros couldn't stay still. He started calling Druckenmiller's office more frequently. Soros and Druckenmiller continued to have heated arguments. As Verisign continued to collapse, Druckenmiller's other bets began to damage the fund even further. His short positions against the S&P 500 and other old-economy companies didn't work out either, which caused the fund to lose even more money. The killing blow came on April 18 when Verisign's stock fell further to $96.

The Quantum Fund was down 22 percent for the year, and its total assets had fallen by $7.6 billion since their peak in 1998 of $22 billion. As he did most days at the Quantum office, Levit greeted Druckenmiller with a "How are you?" at 7:00 a.m.

But this time, the response wasn't as usual. "What do you mean, 'How am I?' We just blew up," Druckenmiller said. By the end of the day, he had handed in his resignation.

Despite being considered one of the all-time great investors, Druckenmiller made the mistake of trusting someone else's judgment over his own. The price he paid for deviating from his own conviction was giving up control of one of the largest hedge funds of that era.

Strategies for Improving Your Judgment

Judgment is the process of evaluating and weighing available information and options to arrive at a reasoned and informed decision. To be a good investor, you need good judgment, because the future is unknown and you need to make decisions with the information you have.

In his early years at Quantum, Stanley Druckenmiller made one good decision after another. He relied on his own judgment and was confident enough that he demanded Soros step away. But a decade later, he stopped relying on himself. When tech stocks were going up, he should've listened to his initial judgment and stayed away.

In March 1999, as the market surged, Druckenmiller expressed his concerns internally to the Quantum team, saying, "I don't like this market. I think we should probably lighten up. I don't want to go out like Steinhardt." He was referring to Michael Steinhardt, a renowned hedge fund manager who ended his long career in 1995 following substantial losses the year prior.

It's evident that Druckenmiller was opposed to engaging in the tech stock bubble. He was aware that the bubble was bound to burst; he just couldn't predict when. Feeling the pressure to salvage the Quantum Fund's returns, he ultimately decided to hire another individual and delegate his decisions about tech stocks. Druckenmiller ignored his own judgment, and the fund ended up participating in the bubble.

Correct judgment is the most important area of philosophy and investing, because it's what helps us to be self-sufficient and consistent. So what is *correct* judgment to a Stoic? It simply means keeping the principles of Stoicism in mind when you make decisions. The following three Stoic strategies will help you to strengthen your judgment.

STRATEGY 1: AIM FOR PURE JUDGMENT

The investor Charlie Munger once said, "The idea of caring that someone is making money faster [than you are] is one of the deadly sins. Envy is a really stupid sin, because it's the only one you could never possibly have any fun at. There's a lot of pain and no fun. Why would you want to get on that trolley?" But inside the offices of the Quantum Fund in 1999 and 2000, they couldn't ignore the pull to get on the trolley.

You will not find another investor with the humility and self-awareness of Druckenmiller, who eventually realized that he had made the wrong judgment in betting big on tech. Ten days after resigning, Druckenmiller said, "It would have been nice to go out on top, like Michael Jordan, but I overplayed my hand."

He got emotional and took risks he normally wouldn't take. The Stoics believed we must separate our emotions from our judgment. They said there are two types of judgment:

1. **Value judgment:** when you let emotions influence your judgment.
2. **Pure judgment:** when you make a rational judgment, free of emotions.

How do we make pure judgments? One of the most famous Marcus Aurelius quotes is this: "Choose not to be harmed—and you won't feel harmed. Don't feel harmed—and you haven't been." If you *say* you've been harmed, you'll feel the harm. If you can ignore harm, seeing the facts for what they are without your emotions interfering, you're making a pure judgment.

Here's what that could look like in daily life. Imagine you just had a performance review at your job, which didn't go as you expected. Your boss gave you negative feedback. That evening you go home and tell your partner, "I received a hurtful review today." Aurelius said we should drop the emotion and instead say, "I received a review today."

Relying on your opinions makes you blind to the facts and realities of the market, which is a common mistake many investors make. For example, you might be convinced that a particular industry is going to be the next big thing, so you

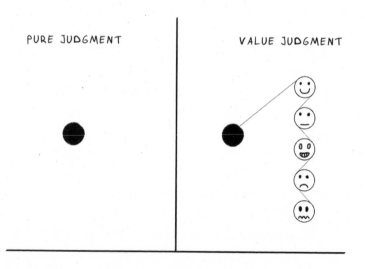

Figure 10: A pure judgment is rational and free of emotion. A value judgment always comes with an opinion or feeling attached to it.

invest heavily in several companies, or buy an ETF, within that industry. But a while later, as companies within the industry publish their quarterly earnings, you see a significant decline in profits. What's worse, the companies give negative forecasts and don't expect to become profitable anytime soon. This bad news drags down the stock prices of the companies you invested in. You were too focused on your optimistic opinion of the industry's future and not focused enough on the facts.

This is what happened to the blockchain industry in 2022. Blockchain is technology that allows secure recording and tracking of information without the need for intermediaries. In the previous years, driven by the popularity of cryptocurrencies and decentralized finance, blockchain companies had grown exponentially. But many investors failed to deeply understand that most of these crypto and blockchain companies had no sustainable business model. Popular companies within that industry, like Riot Blockchain, Marathon Digital Holdings, and Coinbase, were down 90 percent or more from their all-time highs in 2022. Instead of looking at the data, many investors were swayed by opinion makers who said that blockchain and crypto would keep growing at the rate they had in 2020 and 2021.

As an investor, it's critical to make pure judgments, based on data and facts, keeping your mindset free of your opinions, emotions, and ego. That's because our opinions can be wrong, but data is always right.

STRATEGY 2: DETACH FROM OUTCOMES

At the foundation of Stoicism is the idea that we don't control outcomes. We can make good decisions that are based on pure judgments, and yet they may lead to bad outcomes. The reverse is also true. Sometimes people make bad decisions that lead to good outcomes.

But as a Stoic, the aim is to make good decisions and to avoid attachment to outcomes. It doesn't mean we ignore potential outcomes. It means that once you make a decision, it's time to let it go. You can't continue to fret about what will happen. And worse, when you've made a good decision that didn't turn out the way you expected, you shouldn't blame yourself.

As Seneca said, "It is tragic for the soul to be apprehensive of the future and wretched in anticipation of wretchedness, consumed with an anxious desire that the objects which give pleasure may remain in its possession to the very end. For such a soul will never be at rest; in waiting for the future it will lose the present blessings which it might enjoy. And there is no difference between grief for something lost and the fear of losing it."

As a Stoic, the goal is to make decisions that are in line with your values. To avoid envy, greed, and fear. And to do everything in your power to ensure a good outcome. But the actual outcome is not up to you. Druckenmiller wanted to go out like Michael Jordan, who went to six NBA finals and won all six of them.

Druckenmiller didn't allow the bad outcome of the dot-com bubble to stop him. All the time he was working for the Quantum Fund, Druckenmiller never gave up ownership of his own fund, Duquesne Capital. When he left Quantum, he focused full time on Duquesne again. With his own fund, he never had a losing year. That includes all the bad years he had with Quantum. That also includes 2008, the year of the global financial crisis.

When we detach from outcomes, we can spend all our time and energy on what's right in front of us. We can make our decisions to the best of our ability and, once we're done, move on without anxiety or regret.

STRATEGY 3: RECOGNIZE WHAT YOU DON'T KNOW

It's easy to identify mistakes and bad behavior when we look at others. But when it's time to look at ourselves, we often look away. Maybe our ego doesn't want to admit that we don't know everything, or maybe it's painful to be honest with ourselves. It's difficult to acknowledge what you don't know. Too often, we take stock tips from other people, and we make a decision without much thought.

Korean Japanese investor Masayoshi Son has a reputation for being a fearless investor. Many of his bets have failed. But he also has several investments that have paid off extremely well, of which Alibaba is the most famous. His $20 million investment in Alibaba Group in 2000 ballooned to $130 billion in value by 2018. No matter how risky his investments look from the outside, he has an investment process. His investment strategy is about understanding new technologies and investing in them before they hit the mainstream.

But even strategic investors make errors. In a conversation with *New York Times* journalist Andrew Ross Sorkin, Masayoshi Son said that one of his friends told him to put 1 percent of his net worth into Bitcoin. So he invested $200 million in Bitcoin to see how he felt about it. And he said: "I was looking at the price every day, it goes up and down. So I said, this is not good. This is something I don't understand. My mindshare is somewhat affected. I'm at least looking five minutes a day at the price, and I said, this is distracting my focus. It may go up later, it may go down later, but I don't want to spend even one minute a day looking at the price. So I said, okay, I will sell at any price. I sold it with a loss. And I feel so much better."

He lost money trading Bitcoin. But at least he could focus his time on his business, which is investing in technology companies. Son had the emotional fortitude to admit he didn't understand Bitcoin, and he accepted the outcome.

When it comes to trusting your judgment, it's key to recognize the limits of your own abilities. There's nothing wrong with that. Even some of the most skilled investors stay away from assets they don't understand. But to stay away from what we don't understand, we must be honest enough with ourselves to admit we don't know everything. This self-awareness paves the way for greater success in the areas where our strength truly lies.

MEDITATE ON THIS . . .

People try to get away from it all—to the country, to the beach, to the mountains. You always wish that you could too. Which is idiotic: you can get away from it anytime you like. . . . Nowhere you can go is more peaceful—more free of interruptions—than your own soul.

—Marcus Aurelius

The purpose of investing in your education and becoming a well-rounded individual is to be able to rely on yourself. Do not avoid the hard money decisions you must make in life.

Aim to become your own decision-maker. The manager of your own money. Even if you hire a financial adviser or wealth-management firm, make it a goal to know as much about investing as the professional you're hiring.

Rely on your self-awareness to identify what you don't know and what you do know. Don't underestimate nor overestimate your abilities as an investor.

Never forget: no one in the world will care as much about your money as you do.

· **CHAPTER SUMMARY** ·

- Look at yourself as an independent thinker. Rely on your own judgment to make decisions. Correct judgment is nothing more than making a decision after careful consideration.
- Make pure judgments. Let your decisions be based on facts. That means making pure judgments that are rational and free of personal opinions.
- Detach from outcomes. The moment you decide something, let go of the outcome. Accept whatever happens—good or bad.
- Recognize what you don't know. Life's too short to know everything about every financial opportunity in the world. Even the best investors in the world don't know about certain investments and assets. Identifying what you don't know will help you to focus on the things you do know.

· 12 ·

Stick to Your Investing Strategy

You can have the greatest investing strategy in the world, but if you don't stick to it, you will not build any wealth. There are hundreds of thousands of assets you can invest in. But what types of assets you choose to invest in will not make you wealthy. Your behavior is the determining factor. On your path to wealth, you will encounter plenty of advice that contradicts your chosen method, and other methods for investing. Your unwavering belief in the path you choose will help you to stay consistent. If you stay steady, you will not only build substantial wealth but will also do better than your peers and better even than most professional money managers.

When Investing in Yourself Pays Off

Mohnish Pabrai grew up in Mumbai, surrounded by poverty. Born in 1964, Pabrai lived in a tiny apartment his family rented for $20 a month. His father, Om Pabrai, was an entrepreneur who went through multiple bankruptcies.

Seeing his father trying and failing was hard, but Mohnish

saw up close how important consistency was. The young Pabrai remembered how his father remained resilient during the constant pressure of bankruptcy: "My father used to say, 'You could put me naked on a rock in the middle of nowhere, and I would start a business.'"

But the optimism didn't pay off immediately. For his entire childhood, Pabrai's family struggled financially. He saw his parents lose every dime they had multiple times. "And when I say losing everything, I mean not having enough money to buy groceries tomorrow, not having money to pay the rent," Pabrai reflected. His tough childhood motivated him to do well in school. Pabrai graduated from high school ranking third in his class.

Once he graduated, his parents expected him to work in the family business. Driven by his good performance in high school, Pabrai had other goals in mind. He didn't want to work for his father, nor did he want to get a degree in his home country. He wanted to study in America because he felt he would have more opportunities to get wealthy. In 1983, he entered Clemson University in South Carolina, where he got a degree in computer engineering. Pabrai did so well in his finance classes that a professor advised him to shift to finance instead of engineering.

But Pabrai didn't want to change the plan he had laid out for himself. He ignored his professor's advice and finished his engineering degree. When he graduated in 1986, he got a job in the R&D department of a network technology provider called Tellabs. Five years into his career, he lost enthusiasm for his work. Soon he realized that it was time for a change. He no longer wanted to be an employee; he wanted to become what he had initially run away from: an entrepreneur.

But he was committed to avoiding his father's path. Instead of quitting his job, a high-risk move, he started his own business, TransTech, on the side. His business offered IT consulting and systems integration to clients. After ten months, Pabrai felt that his new business had enough profit to sustain him financially. And that gave him the confidence to pursue it full time, so he handed in his resignation at Tellabs.

Within six years, in 1996, TransTech was recognized as an Inc. 500 company. By that time, Pabrai had also earned enough money to set aside $1 million in savings. One day, when he was waiting for a flight at Heathrow Airport in London, he bought *One Up on Wall Street* by Peter Lynch. He learned about the power of compounding and having a long-term approach to investing.

Pabrai also learned about Warren Buffett in that book. He was so impressed by the amount of wealth that Buffett had achieved by investing in stocks that he wanted to do the same. After reading Lynch's book, he started reading everything about Warren Buffett and his partner, Charlie Munger. For the rest of the nineties, Pabrai applied the value-investing strategy of Buffett and Munger with success.

As he continued to grow his company, he found that he had become more excited about the stock market than about working on TransTech. One Monday in 1999, Pabrai woke up and didn't feel any excitement about working on the business he had founded himself. TransTech was a mature business with growing revenue.

Pabrai realized that he wanted to devote his time to investing full time, rather than continuing to work on TransTech or starting another business. In 1999, he sold his company, at the height of the tech bubble, for $20 million.

He launched an investment fund, now called Pabrai Funds, with $900,000 from eight people and $100,000 of his own money. Pabrai didn't want to put his entire fortune on the line. While he was confident in his skills and investing strategy, he still moved cautiously.

But taking on other people's money to invest also comes at a price. When investors give you their money, they expect you to give them a return on investment within a year or two. Pabrai, however, was adamant about taking a long-term perspective and strictly followed the rules of value investing.

Pabrai realized that Buffett had achieved good results in his career because he stuck to his strategy. Everyone can learn about value investing by reading Benjamin Graham's book *The Intelligent Investor*. Everyone can also learn about how Buffett invests by reading the countless books that have been written about him. There are no secrets to value investing. One simply identifies undervalued companies, buys their stock, and waits. That last part is the hard part and what usually trips up unsuccessful value investors.

But Pabrai *lived and breathed* value investing. He executed the strategy without diverging by even an inch. He loved the fact that most investors don't stick to a particular strategy. "The good news is, I'm playing against players who don't even fucking know the rules," he said. Pabrai took pride in his ability to execute his investing strategy, which he called Dhandho investing, after the Gujarati word *dhandho*, meaning "wealth."

While Dhandho investing and value investing follow the same method for picking stocks, Dhandho investing has a distinct focus on minimizing risk. This strong focus on minimizing risk while maximizing returns is driven by Pabrai's background. As an immigrant, he feels like he can't afford to take even the slightest amount of risk. While Warren Buffett's firm, Berkshire Hathaway, occasionally invests in tech start-ups like Snowflake, Pabrai exclusively sticks to companies with a long history of success.

Pabrai's strategy proved to be successful despite his low risk tolerance. Pabrai Funds achieved a 1,204 percent return from 2000 to 2018.

Pabrai's investing strategy meant that he had to be strict about saying no. If Pabrai saw a long list of companies and found nothing worth investing in, he'd simply sit back and stick to his current positions. During the 2008 market crash, he invested in ten companies he found to be undervalued. Among these investments were unknown names like Pinnacle Airlines Corp., Air Transport Services, Teck Cominco, and Horsehead Holding, which, despite the crash, returned well over 200 percent from 2008 through 2009. Then he did nothing for three years. In all of 2011, he bought stocks of only two companies, then three in 2012. He bought nothing the following year. He invested in only a few companies the year after, never breaking his main rule of going after low-risk opportunities.

Pabrai showed that anyone can build wealth if they are persistent. He didn't take much risk, nor did he have some kind of unique investing strategy. He took the value-investing strategy, put an emphasis on minimizing risk, and executed that strategy flawlessly.

How to Follow Through on Your Plan

The most important factor that determines your success is consistent execution. Epictetus said: "Once you undertake to do something, stick with it and treat it as something that should be carried through. Don't pay attention to what people say. It should not influence you in any way."

Consistency is what defines investing success. The type of strategy you use is less important than whether you can stay the course and execute it to perfection. The truth is that there are only a handful of proven investing strategies, and they have been publicly known for decades:

1. **Technical analysis and momentum trading** took off in the early 1900s with traders like Jesse Livermore. Technical analysis involves using past market data to identify trends and patterns. Traders scrutinize historical price data to predict future movements.

2. **Fundamental investing** started to take off with the introduction of value investing by Benjamin Graham in the 1930s. Fundamental investing focuses on analyzing a company's financials and other economic factors to determine its long-term intrinsic value and potential for growth. Growth investing is a form of fundamental investing where the focus is on companies that exhibit strong potential for growth in the future.

3. **Quantitative investing** became popular with the work of Edward Thorp in the 1970s. Quantitative investing involves using mathematical models, statistical analysis, and other sophisticated computational techniques to identify investment opportunities in the market.

4. **Passive investing** was introduced in the late 1970s, largely because of the work of John Bogle. It involves investing in a diversified portfolio of stocks or bonds that tracks a particular index, with the goal of achieving market returns with low fees and minimal effort.

That's it. And yet people publish hundreds of new books every year that claim to have the key to beating the market. Every one of those books proposes a "new" strategy, which is in fact a different take on an existing framework.

Investors who failed to achieve success assume that there's something wrong with their strategy. They quickly decide they need a different strategy as soon as they don't get the results they want. Those investors are served by thousands of people in the finance industry who make a living by selling information products that claim to have the secret to consistently beating the market.

Howard Marks warned against people who try to trick investors in his book *Mastering the Market Cycle*: "I've seen dozens of silver bullets touted over the course of my 48-year career. Not one has proved out. No investment strategy or tactic will ever deliver a high return without risk, especially to buyers lacking a high level of investing skill." If there were silver bullets and other successful investing strategies, we all would know about them.

Successful investing is not about figuring out what strategy is best; it's about staying committed to a strategy that works. To make sure you follow through on your plan through bull and bear markets, apply the following strategies to your life.

1. IGNORE THE NOISE.

In the year 1999, stock market news dominated mainstream newspapers. Tech stocks were so popular that the famous tech exchange Nasdaq paid $37 million for an eight-story video screen in the heart of Times Square. According to a *New York Times* article published on December 29, 1999, the sign "was designed to give the stock market a public face in the global market that can compete with its better-known rival, the New York Stock Exchange." Millions of Americans were enamored with tech stocks, which were heavily covered by mainstream media. Three months after the *Times* article was published, the dot-com bubble started to burst.

Pabrai ignored the chatter about how great technology stocks were. Instead, he looked at investors like Peter Lynch and Warren Buffett because they had a framework—a strategy they applied for decades. That's what Pabrai was attracted to, not the high-flying stocks of that time.

To be long-term investors, we must be able to distinguish the signal from the noise. You can't open social media without stumbling upon stock market tips or warnings. When there's a bull market, the stock market geniuses will try to convince you they have the key to beating the market. When there's a bear market, the same genius has the blueprint for surviving the next crash. The fact is no one can predict the market with full certainty, not even the most seasoned investors. Ignore anyone who is foolish enough to say they can.

2. COMPARE YOURSELF WITH PEOPLE WHO DON'T INVEST.

Ideally, we shouldn't compare ourselves with others. But the Stoics realized that we can't avoid our human tendencies. We look at people who are wealthier or spend more, and we think, *I want that life.* Those types of thoughts can push us off our path.

The problem is that when you deviate from your plan, you can do serious harm to your long-term prospects for building wealth. If you get enticed by a get-rich-quick-scheme and decide to put 50 percent of your wealth on the line, and you lose a big chunk of it, you might have to work for years to recoup those losses.

When you notice that you are starting to compare yourself with others, try a mental trick that Seneca taught his friend Lucilius in a letter he wrote him. Seneca advises against looking at the people who might be better, smarter, or more accomplished than you. Instead, Seneca recommends, "continually remind yourself . . . of the many things you have achieved. When you look at all the people out in front of you, think of all the ones behind you."

If you insist on comparing yourself with others, compare yourself with *all* people—not only the ultrasuccessful. No matter where you are in life, there are always people who don't have some of the things you do have. That awareness will help remind you to appreciate what you have and what you've already accomplished.

3. SET FINANCIAL GOALS THAT ARE WITHIN YOUR CONTROL.

Mohnish Pabrai is famous for having only a few stocks in his portfolio. As of July 2023, he had only three positions, one of which, Micron Technology, represented 77 percent of his entire portfolio.

He's very selective about the stocks he buys, and when he does, he invests large sums. Pabrai's investment process revolves around setting goals that are within his control. Instead of aiming for a certain amount of return on investment, he focuses on the time he spends on research.

We must be brutally honest about our expectations for building wealth. It might sound nice to retire at forty, but if we don't earn hundreds of thousands of dollars a year in our twenties and thirties, it's not realistic. Especially considering that most people earn more when they are in their forties and fifties. Those are your peak earning years.

We need to look at how much we are earning at any given moment and how much we can realistically set aside to invest. Instead of looking at dollar values, like "I want to invest $20K a year," it's better to think in percentages.

Saving or investing 30 percent of your net income is a great goal. That leaves you the rest to spend on daily necessities and fun. In some phases of our lives, we can't save that much, so we can aim for 10 percent. If you can't save 10 percent, it's worth downgrading your lifestyle and saving more.

No matter what your financial goal ends up being, focus on the aspects of investing that you can control:

1. **Discretionary spending:** This refers to all nonessential items, like recreation and entertainment.
2. **Effort:** This is the amount of time and energy you spend on your work and personal education. The more skills you acquire, the more value you can provide in the marketplace.
3. **Consistency:** We can choose to keep going and to maintain a constant practice of saving and investing, even when it doesn't seem worthwhile in the short term.

Juvenal once said, "All wish to possess knowledge, but few, comparatively speaking, are willing to pay the price." The price we pay for a wealthier future is that we put some money aside today. That doesn't sound like a bad deal to me.

MEDITATE ON THIS...

If you accomplish something good with hard work, the labor passes quickly, but the good endures; if you do something shameful in pursuit of pleasure, the pleasure passes quickly, but the shame endures.

—Musonius Rufus

Think about a time you quit a tough project or chose the easy way over learning something new. How did you feel afterward? It's likely that you didn't feel great.

Contrast that with a time you accomplished something important that required tedious work. Finishing a project, getting a degree, moving abroad, starting a business, making art, creating a tree house for your kids.

These are the accomplishments that make you feel proud after the fact. The sense of accomplishment you get from finishing hard things is unmatched. Focus on these activities over the former.

· CHAPTER SUMMARY ·

- Execution makes you wealthy, not your strategy. Many investors are always looking for the perfect strategy that can make them more money. But there's no perfect strategy. Instead, aim for perfect execution of a good investing strategy.
- Focus on your own actions. People will always brag about how much money they've generated with stocks. Ignore the stories. It's just noise.
- Compare yourself with people who aren't investing. When you look at people who are wealthier than you, don't forget to also look at people who have less wealth.
- Set financial goals you control. Aim to save or invest a specific percentage of your income every month. Once you set the percentage, stick to it as much as you can.

Stoic Investing Techniques

· 13 ·

How to Start Investing
in Stocks

Seneca's life was characterized by two phases. During the first phase of his life, he became educated, moved to the capital of the Western world, Rome, and enjoyed a long career in politics. The second phase of his life started when he was sixty-two and decided to retreat from the hectic Roman lifestyle. By that time, he had built substantial wealth, so he could afford to travel to some of the most beautiful places in Italy.

In our modern-day lives, we aim to follow the same structure. Dedicate the first phase of your life to getting educated, earning a living, and building wealth. This stage of your life is often described as the wealth-accumulation phase, which is followed by the retirement phase. Most financial planners agree that we should invest differently depending on whether we're in the wealth-accumulation phase or the retirement phase. There isn't an exact age when you move from one phase to the other—you may be sixty-two, like Seneca, or not.

In this chapter I'll cover the Stoic investing strategy I propose during the wealth-accumulation phase (in the next chapter we'll dive into the retirement phase).

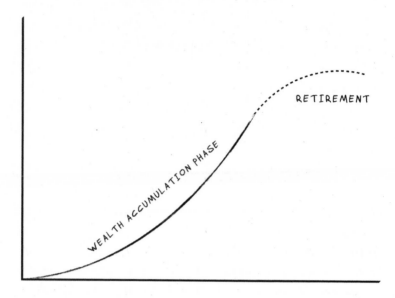

Figure 11: The wealth-accumulation phase of our lives constitutes the largest part of our lifetimes. Our focus during this phase is on building wealth. When we retire, the focus is on living off the money we have, and it's no longer a priority to grow our wealth.

How to Invest during the Wealth-Accumulation Phase

We've spent a lot of time on philosophy in this book because it's the key to investing success. But we also need to be practical. Let's get down to it.

If you're completely new to investing in stocks, make sure you have an emergency fund before you start. This is a quantity of money set aside in a risk-free place, ideally a high-yield savings account. Six months' worth of expenses is a good rule of thumb. That fund will help you to avoid financial turmoil in the face of unexpected situations. Under no circumstances should you invest in stocks with money that you need for your expenses and cost of living.

Next you need to decide what you should invest in with the money you can put aside for long-term investing. I hope I've answered that throughout this book. By investing in an S&P 500 index fund, you will have direct exposure to the broader stock market and you'll profit from economic growth. As the economy grows, your stock portfolio grows. This is the perfect strategy to get started because it takes almost no time. You can get as sophisticated and active as you want later. For now, focus only on *starting*.

In terms of capital allocation, here's what I recommend: invest 100 percent in U.S. stocks. At least at the beginning. When you're just getting started, you don't need to diversify your portfolio by owning international stocks or get complicated by owning other asset classes. You can keep it simple by just putting all the money you want to invest in an S&P 500 index fund.

Avoid bonds. (They have a lower return; more on that in the next chapter.) Avoid buying rental properties. It takes time and energy to close deals, and real estate historically has underperformed stocks. This doesn't mean you should never invest in bonds or real estate. If circumstances call for it, you might want to invest in other asset classes.

Now it's time to open a brokerage account or retirement account so you can finally get started. The best way is by opening a 401(k) retirement savings account through your employer so you can make use of tax benefits. You can ask your HR department about what this entails. In 2023, you can contribute $22,500 (or up to $30,000 if you're older than fifty) to this account.

This contribution is tax deferred, which means it's deducted from your pretax salary, so you pay less income tax. Some employers match your contributions up to a certain amount, which gives your retirement account a decent boost.

Most employer-sponsored retirement accounts offer at least

one S&P 500 index fund. The maximum contribution for a 401(k) is enough for most people, so you don't need additional tax-advantaged accounts like an IRA. If you're self-employed, you can sign up for a solo 401(k) account at whatever brokerage you prefer. I recommend Vanguard.

If you're outside the U.S., check whether your country offers tax-deferred investing through your employer. If that's not available, you can purchase an S&P 500 ETF (search for the ticker symbol VOO if you're in the U.S. or VUSA if you're in Europe) through a brokerage account and hold it either in an individual retirement account (if applicable) or a taxable account.

Interactive Brokers is a solid stockbroker that is available in over two hundred countries. It's the one I use. Like most modern brokers, IBKR also offers automated investing. Once you set it up, you will automatically invest the same amount each month.

The most important thing is to keep your method of investing in stocks so simple that you can't use any excuses. I am sure that you now know enough to get started with investing in stocks. You only need to ask yourself, *With how much?*

How Much You Need to Invest

In chapter 12, I mentioned that saving 30 percent of your net income is a great goal. If you can't save that much, adjust it downward, with a minimum of 10 percent. But does that mean all your savings, outside your emergency fund, should go to the stock market? What if you want to save money for buying a house or getting a higher degree? Should you invest all your savings in the stock market and pull it out when you need it?

I don't recommend withdrawing any money from your portfolio during the entire wealth-accumulation phase. If you want to save for a big purchase or getting a degree, use your savings account and then allocate less money to the stock market. Let's say you can save 30 percent. Put 20 percent of that money in your savings account that you dedicate to your big purchase, and use 10 percent to buy an S&P 500 ETF. Even if you invest small sums, it's worth it.

Before you think you need to invest thousands of dollars a month so you end up with millions when you retire, let's do the math with a median household income of $80,893 a year. The take-home pay would be roughly $57,000. And let's use the average annualized return of the S&P 500 since 1980 of 11.44 percent.

- Investing 10 percent a year, or $5,700, over 30 years results in $1,246,764.61.
- Investing 20 percent a year, or $11,400, over 30 years results in $2,493,529.23.
- Investing 30 percent a year, or $17,100, over 30 years results in $3,740,293.84.

Keep in mind that this quick calculation reflects investing outside retirement accounts. If you invest the same amounts in your 401(k) account, you will pay less tax, which means your take-home income will be higher. Either way, all the above options are enough to retire on.

The question is: How comfortable do you want to be when you retire? If you want to be *really* comfortable, you need the last option. It may not be realistic to aim for investing 30 percent of your income during periods of life with more expenses, but you can still aim to invest *something*. Even with a lower amount you can build substantial wealth over time.

If you don't have time on your side, you'll need to invest more. If we shorten the horizon to fifteen years, you'll need to invest roughly $32,000 a year. But because most of us earn more in our forties and fifties, it's still a realistic goal. We might need to invest 30 percent to 50 percent of our income. There are people who already do that in their twenties, which is unnecessary. Life is too short to deprive yourself too much. Balance is the key.

And then there are two other factors that can also have a positive impact on your financial situation later in life. Keep the following things in mind about retirement:

- **You probably will receive Social Security checks.** The average retired U.S. worker received $1,830 each month in 2023. The government ensures that Social Security checks keep up with inflation. But in recent years they have outpaced inflation. For example, retired workers received $1,164 in 2010. In 2023 retirees saw a 57 percent increase from 2010 levels, whereas consumer prices increased by 38 percent during that time.

- **You might have paid off your mortgage and have a lower cost of living.** In 2022, 66 percent of U.S. households were living in a house they owned. While many people assume that younger generations have trouble buying houses, the data contradict this. In 2022, around 30 percent of twenty-five-year-olds, who belong to Gen Z (born between 1997 to 2013), owned a home. This percentage is slightly higher than the 28 percent of millennials (born between 1981 and 1996) and the 27 percent of Gen Xers (born between 1965 and 1980) who owned a home.

Now, buying a house and living in it is not a substitute for investing in stocks. You won't be able to profit from an increase in property value until you sell your home at a higher price. And buying or selling a home comes with costs, which eat away your potential returns. For these reasons, it's best to view homeownership as a long-term commitment to live somewhere instead of a way to build wealth.

Even if your Social Security checks are lower and you don't own a house, it's not an issue. In fact, that's one of the reasons you're investing in the stock market—to mitigate the risks of relying on government support and homeownership. You invest because you want to be independent. So look at Social Security and homeownership as bonuses that could make retirement more comfortable.

Do You Need an Adviser?

If you decide to use a human financial adviser or a robo-adviser, you have to take those costs into account. Financial advisers typically charge 1 percent or more per year of assets under management. Most robo-advisers charge between 0.2 percent and 0.5 percent a year.

I believe a human financial adviser is beneficial when you have a seven-figure portfolio or when you're over fifty. When you have a lot of money at stake or when you're nearing retirement, the feeling of fear gets magnified by 10X when there's a bear market. During those moments, a financial adviser can be worth the 1 percent they typically charge.

When the market crashes and you think, *Oh no! I'm down*

$300K. How can I ever come back from this? I need to stop the bleeding, you can use someone who reminds you that losses are permanent only when you sell. That type of emotional support is something a robo-adviser or online stockbroker can't provide. Those platforms will execute any order you give them. Your human adviser will take the time to talk to you before you make a move.

But when you're in the prime of the wealth-accumulation phase of your life, you need to save on costs. Plus, you should be too busy living your life to think about selling your equities.

If you're not an investment professional but you're looking at what the market does every single day, you're doing something wrong with your life. Go and enjoy! Build a career. Start a family. Spend time with your friends. And keep investing along the way.

• CHAPTER SUMMARY •

- Allocate 100 percent to stocks during the wealth-accumulation phase. This strategy has the best risk/reward ratio. And it doesn't require much time.
- Invest at least 10 percent of your net income, ideally 30 percent. Find your ideal number by looking at your lifestyle. If you can't invest enough for several years, invest more in the subsequent years.
- Don't deprive yourself. Investing $5,700 a year for thirty years will make you a millionaire if the annual return remains 11.44 percent.
- Avoid high fees. Small costs incurred over decades will lead to huge dollar amounts in missed returns. Watch your costs and fees carefully.

· 14 ·

Retire Like a Stoic

The conventional wisdom has been that in retirement, one should have more exposure to bonds than to stocks. The idea is that bonds are safer and usually have a return that's equal to inflation, or slightly higher. Bonds should help you to preserve wealth once you retire.

From 1928 to 2022, U.S. Treasury bonds had an average yearly return of 4.87 percent. The stock market returned roughly 10 percent a year on average in that same time frame. When you invest in bonds, in the best case, you're giving up around 5 percent of returns so you have less volatility. Ultimately, that's what it comes down to: bonds don't have the wild swings of the stock market.

But as a Stoic investor, you can take the volatility of the stock market even when you retire. After all, volatility is the price you pay for potentially higher returns. If you own only bonds, you aren't necessarily safer, and you won't accumulate much wealth. Think about your margin of safety when it comes to your returns and inflation.

If inflation is 3 percent, your margin of safety is 7 percent when you're in stocks and only 1.87 percent when you're in bonds. That doesn't sound safe to me, especially when inflation is higher.

Here's the reason why stocks outperform bonds. When someone buys a bond, they are essentially lending money to the bond issuer, whether it's a government, corporation, or other entity. In exchange, the bondholder receives interest payments and the promise that the principal amount will be repaid at a future date, known as the bond's maturity date. As a lender, the bondholder has more security than a shareholder or owner because they have a legal contract that guarantees repayment of the principal amount.

However, unlike stockholders, bondholders don't get a piece of profits or dividends if a business performs well. As a bondholder, you can never enjoy the upside of economic growth. As a stockholder you get all the upside, but in return, you have more volatility. That doesn't mean you have much more risk. If a corporation goes bust and you own its bonds, there's still a chance you won't get all your money back.

For these reasons, having exposure to stocks is still better for preserving and building wealth during retirement because it simply has much better returns at a slightly higher level of risk. If you do want to have less volatility, opt for a 60/40 portfolio, where you allocate 60 percent to stocks and 40 percent to bonds.

How and When to Withdraw Money

When it comes to withdrawal rate (the amount you sell every year in retirement to live off), financial experts often talk about the "X% rule." The most used percentage is 4 percent. But withdrawal rates shouldn't be strict—they should be like life: fluid. A person who strictly lives by the 4 percent rule will deprive themselves when they actually need to withdraw 6 percent in a year. On the other side, they might end up taking out money they don't need when they need only 2 percent in another year.

It's important to stay flexible when you retire. Seneca said it best: "We should also make ourselves flexible, so that we do not pin our hopes too much on our set plans." What's important during retirement is the following:

Calculate how much money you need to live on every month.

Consider Social Security checks or other retirement income you might have.

Withdraw the extra money you need from your 401(k) or individual brokerage account *every month* (don't withdraw a year's worth of expenses all at once). For example, if you need $3,000 a month, sell that amount in stocks on the first working day of every month.

Still keep six months' worth of savings in a dedicated savings account to avoid emergency selling of your stocks.

There's nothing wrong with withdrawing 6 percent in a year when the stock market is up 10 percent. It's also okay if you only withdraw 3 to 4 percent in a year when stocks are down.

With your knowledge of the stock market and how investing works, you can adapt your withdrawal rate based on market conditions. But avoid spending too much time and energy on diversification or minimizing risk. It's simply not worth your effort to get the same return with less volatility. As a Stoic investor your edge is that you're immune to volatility.

Avoid Living in the Future

One of the biggest causes of sorrow in life is when you wake up one day and think, *Why didn't I do the things I wanted to do earlier in life?* This is something I've seen with every single member of my family as they went into their sixties.

As Seneca says, "You will hear many people saying: 'When I am fifty I shall retire into leisure; when I am sixty I shall give up public duties.' And what guarantee do you have of a longer life?"

You can save, invest, and plan all you want, but you have no guarantee of a long life. Live a responsible life. Have an eye on the future, but live today. Most of us do the reverse. In our minds we live in the future, and as a result, we pay too little attention to the present. We tell ourselves to put off enjoyment until we earn a certain salary, receive a promotion, get a degree, find love, and so forth.

Most people are only ready to "live just when life must end," as Seneca beautifully said. When they stare death in the eye, they realize that life is short. As you go through life, never forget that the future isn't guaranteed. Stick to your plans. But never wait for the perfect future moment to start living. Life happens right here. Right now.

• **CHAPTER SUMMARY** •

- If you want to maximize returns during retirement, stay 100 percent in stocks. As a Stoic investor, you're used to the ups and downs of the market. If you want to have the highest possible returns without taking excessive risk, stay the course.

- If you're a more defensive retiree, allocate 60 percent to stocks and 40 percent to bonds. With this portfolio your returns will be lower, but you'll have more peace of mind if market swings bother you.
- Withdraw the amount of money you need each month. Avoid selling stocks to withdraw a whole year's worth of expenses.
- While you're investing, don't think about retirement too much. When you're diligently investing every month, you know your wealth will be fine by the time you retire.

· 15 ·

The 90/10 Rule of Speculation

Most books about passive investing and personal finance are resolutely against trading stocks. They argue that it can't be done, because most stock market traders and hedge fund managers fail to beat the market. They extrapolate that conclusion and assume that no one can beat the market. This is obviously not true. The truth is that beating the market is extremely hard and too time-consuming. After all, that's why I propose in this book to use a simple investing strategy.

But if you're curious about active trading and you're willing to put in the work, you can earn a profit. Just because the odds are against you doesn't mean it can't be done. As Marcus Aurelius once said: "If a thing is difficult to be accomplished by thyself, do not think that it is impossible for man: but if anything is possible for man and conformable to his nature, think that this can be attained by thyself too."

Ever since I learned about the stock market, I've loved the idea of trading. As I grew older and got to know myself better, I learned that I'm not a big risk taker, so I limit my trades. I follow the 90/10 rule of speculation:

Cap your losses by speculating with only 10 percent of your total stock portfolio.

This rule allows me to pursue higher-risk trades but ensures that I'll never go too far. For every dollar I put in the stock market, I dedicate 90 cents to the S&P 500 index. That money goes into the market and stays there for a long time. Then I use the other 10 cents to speculate. Maybe I'll turn the 10 cents into 20 cents, and maybe I'll lose it all. Both outcomes are fine.

Remember, trading and investing are two different disciplines. Investing means buying and holding stocks. Trading (or speculating) is the process of buying and selling, intending to make a profit on your trades. A good trader is often not a good long-term investor, because it requires a different skill set. The reverse is also true. But that doesn't mean investors never trade, or vice versa.

Even the most famous long-term investor, Warren Buffett, occasionally trades stocks. While Buffett aims to buy and hold stocks, sometimes they end up as short-term trades. For example, in 2020, Berkshire Hathaway bought shares of the gold-mining company Barrick Gold and sold the shares six months later at almost the same price, roughly breaking even on the trade.

The position represented a minuscule 0.064 percent of Berkshire's total assets, so the company's risk was minimal. As individual investors, we don't have billions of dollars to invest, so we need to allocate a higher percentage to trading if we want to make it worthwhile.

If you trade with 50 percent of your savings and you lose it all, your lifestyle has to change. You will have less financial security, and that impacts the way you live. If you trade with 1 percent of your savings and you lose it, you're fine. But even if you post a 100 percent return, the extra money you earn will not be worth it, relatively speaking.

Let's say you have $100,000 and you speculate with $1,000. A 20 percent return on that is $200, which is fine but only 0.2 percent of your total portfolio. If you speculate with $10,000 and achieve the same return, you just made $2,000, which makes your effort worth it. Remember that earning that return requires significant time and energy.

If you don't speculate with larger amounts of money (but still small enough amounts that you won't miss), it's simply not worth the time. So if you want to trade stocks but you have less than $10,000, it's not a good investment of your time. It makes more sense when your potential returns are more than what you make at your job.

Either way, the 90/10 rule is the most responsible and Stoic approach to speculation. You limit your potential loss, and your potential returns will be worth your time.

Over the past decade, I've studied the most successful stock market traders, like Jesse Livermore, Stanley Druckenmiller, George Soros, Paul Tudor Jones, Richard Dennis, Sir John Templeton, Marty Schwartz, and many more. Based on their results and ideas, I've extracted five pillars of successful stock market trading.

Pillar 1: Trade Infrequently

The best traders in history were not day traders. Instead, they made several successful trades every year. Sometimes they would avoid trading altogether, when the market went against them. And other times they would trade more because they saw more opportunities.

Overall, it's a misconception that successful traders make

a bunch of trades every single day. As Jesse Livermore said, "Money cannot consistently be made trading every day or every week during the year."

The most money is made by traders who buy when the market is coming out of a correction or a bottom. In his book *Devil Take the Hindmost*, Edward Chancellor writes about how some of the early traders made money in the 1860s by following the "panic bird" strategy: "Some speculators, known as 'panic birds,' came to the market only once prices had crashed and money was scarce; they bought carefully, locked up their investments, and kept away from Wall Street until the next calamity struck."

In a similar way, the traders who picked up stocks in the aftermath of the financial crisis of 2008 made big returns. But as Chancellor warns, the panic birds were a "rare breed." It requires discipline and patience to trade only when you see exceptional opportunities.

Pillar 2: Cap Your Losses at 10 Percent

Because stock trading is a complex pursuit, it's likely that a trader will have more losing trades than winning trades. The good traders simply earn a big return when they're right and limit their losses when they're wrong.

Successful traders cap their losses to avoid blowing up their accounts. A good trader is not afraid to be wrong. When you buy an asset as a short-term trader, you expect it to go up. If that doesn't happen within two weeks or so, you were wrong. A good trader quickly admits that when time is up and gets out.

The best way to do that is to think about when you want to get out of a trade before you enter it. A common loss threshold is 10 percent.

When you buy a stock, you can immediately set a stop-loss order at 10 percent. A stop-loss is an order you can place that will go through only when your stock drops below a specified level. Let's say you purchase a stock at $100 per share, and you want to cap your loss at 10 percent. You set a stop-loss order at $90 per share. If the price falls to $90 or below, the stop-loss order will be triggered, and the security will automatically be sold at the market price.

Pillar 3: Never Average Down

When you ignore the previous pillar, you tend to double down on your wrong call. This is called averaging down, and it's a form of self-deception. A trader who buys a stock at $100 with the expectation that it will go up to $130 will have a hard time getting out of the trade if the price goes lower. Indeed, they might even want to buy more. After all, if you like a stock at $100, you should love it at $80—the market is giving you a temporary discount.

But that's how a long-term investor should think, not a trader. If you're trading stocks, get out if the stock goes the other way. Here's how the self-deception happens.

Let's say you buy a stock at $100, and it goes to $80. You ignore pillar 2 and buy one more share at $80, which brings your average cost down to $90 per share. Great, you'll get a better return when you go from $90 to $130. But that's the wrong assumption. As every trader and investor must acknowledge, the market does what it wants. The $80 stock could go to $200, but it could also go to $20. Do you want to risk the latter? Cut your losses before they spiral out of control.

Pillar 4: Don't Buy Popular Assets

When people talk about a certain stock or asset at school, during your lunch break at work, or at birthday parties, it's too late to buy. The prices of all new and trendy stocks follow a cycle:

1. **Obscurity:** When only a small community knows about a new trend, technology, or company that's growing fast.
2. **Awareness:** The moment cognizant investors find out and start buying heavily. Some financial outlets pick up on the trend.
3. **Euphoria:** Mainstream and social media talk about the big returns on a certain asset. This is when noninvestors get curious and start buying. This is also when the serious investors start selling.
4. **Collapse:** Without the serious investors, the demand for the asset collapses and the late-stage investors end up holding the bag.

It sounds great to buy during stages 1 and 2, but in reality, that might happen only a handful of times during the lifetime of a professional investor. You're better off trying to avoid buying during the end of stage 3. That's when news outlets like *The New York Times* and CNBC have picked up on something or when your friends who are not investors talk about a particular stock or asset. But through your own research and screening of stocks, you could run into opportunities in late stage 2 or *early* stage 3, which is not too late to generate a profit. Just get out once you've made a profit.

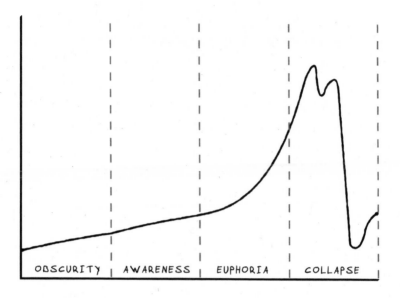

OBSCURITY | AWARENESS | EUPHORIA | COLLAPSE

Figure 12: Prices of new and trendy stocks follow a common pattern that's linked to the overall psychology of the market.

Pillar 5: 20 Percent Profit Is Enough

The biggest threat to a trader is getting too greedy. When I started trading stocks, I was up 30 percent or more many times. But I would always think, *What if this goes higher and I miss out on even more profit?*

Inevitably, the stock would decline and I would tell myself it was only temporary and keep holding. The stock would keep declining. Finally, after far too long, I would sell it at a loss. This is why trading stocks is so confusing. You think, *What happened? I was up 30 percent and now I'm down 30 percent?*

That's how fast the market moves. If you want to be a serious trader, you need a strategy for taking profit. Will you sometimes miss out on ten baggers? Sure. But at least you make money and avoid big losses.

As soon as I have more than 20 percent profit on a trade, I sell it outright if I don't trust the price will keep rising. If I feel like the stock has more upside potential, I use a "trailing stop-loss" order to protect my profit as the price keeps going up. Unlike a regular stop-loss order, a trailing order automatically adjusts your stop-loss price as the stock price rises. For example, if you bought a stock at $100 and it goes to $140, you can do three things:

1. Sell it at $140 and take 40 percent profit.
2. Keep the stock and set a stop-loss at $120 to establish your 20 percent profit and also give the stock room to go up.
3. Set a trailing-stop loss at 10 percent, to see whether the stock will go up more but at the same time ensure you get no less than 20 percent profit.

If your stock rises to $140, your trailing stop-loss of 10 percent means the stock will be sold at $126. If the price moves to $150, the trailing stop is at $135. This 10 percent margin will keep trailing the market price, which means you can make more money. Using this strategy will help you to avoid the regret of selling a stock that keeps going up. You should always focus on the profit you've put in your pocket, not the imaginary one that you only think or talk about.

A Game of Discipline, Skill, or Luck

The stock market can be three things: a long-term wealth generator, a marketplace, or a casino. Here's what each one means for what you want from the market.

1. **Long-term wealth generator:** You don't want to spend time on investing. But you still want to build wealth. Hence, you need a Stoic discipline to stay invested through the ups and downs.
2. **A marketplace:** You look at the stock market as a place to buy and sell goods. In a way, you operate your trading account as a business. Your products are assets. You need capital to operate your business. As in any other business you operate, you need skill.
3. **A casino:** You don't want to spend time or energy learning about the stock market. You just want to take a shot. Maybe you'll get rich.

As a Stoic, it's important to be brutally honest with yourself. What's your approach to the stock market? If you demonstrate even a hint of gambling, of buying and selling stocks without a strategy, admit it to yourself. Understand you will probably never make money gambling on stocks, just like the gambler who goes to Las Vegas.

If you want to be dead serious about trading, and you look at it like you're operating a business, trading could work for you. Even if you want to trade with 10 percent of your money and trade relatively few times. Do it well, or don't do it at all.

The Stoics believed in giving every task you do your best. As Marcus Aurelius said: "Concentrate every minute like a Roman . . . on doing what's in front of you with precise and genuine seriousness, tenderly, willingly, with justice."

If you don't plan to be serious about trading, avoid trading altogether. Simply use the stock market as a way of building long-term wealth by following the passive-investing strategy laid out in this book.

• CHAPTER SUMMARY •

- Trading stocks is different from investing in stocks. Think carefully before you start trading stocks. It's a discipline that requires different skills from investing.
- If you want to trade stocks, be disciplined. A stock-trading strategy can be successful only if you stick to it religiously. Otherwise, it becomes a way to lose money.
- Be serious about making a profit. If you're consistently losing money trading stocks, rethink your strategy or quit. The goal of trading is to make money.

Conclusion

Be Like Granite

There was once a king who had the ability to turn every-thing he touched into gold. After helping out a lost satyr (a character from Greek mythology that was known for chasing pleasure and being a follower of Dionysus, the god of wine and ecstasy), King Midas received an offer from Diony-sus as a sign of gratitude. Dionysus said he would fulfill any one wish Midas had. Midas, greedy as he was, wished that everything he touched would turn into gold.

Midas walked away happier than ever. He started touch-ing random objects, and exactly as he had wished, everything turned to gold. But soon enough, he realized that he hadn't thought things through. How would the king ever eat? He turned to his daughter and hugged her in despair, and—poof!—she turned into a gold statue. Full of regret, he went back to Dionysus and begged to reverse his wish.

I learned about King Midas as a kid in school. Back then, Midas was still used as a cautionary tale, just the way it was intended. But in today's world, the phrase "Midas touch" is used in a *positive* way. When someone has the Midas touch, they are good at making money.

As you follow the Stoic path to wealth, don't forget the

lesson of King Midas: more doesn't lead to freedom. Social media makes us envious of others' new cars, houses, exotic vacations. So many of us feel like we're missing out and that everyone else is living better. These negative emotions are your biggest enemy as you build wealth.

To apply everything we covered in this book—and we covered a lot of ground—we must stay Stoic during our entire lifetime, which means keeping our emotions in check. If you live by the Stoic path, you will resist your negative emotions and stay consistent. You will do the following:

1. **Invest in yourself:** With your knowledge and skills, you will always be able to provide value in the economy. You don't have to fear being without income for long.

2. **Accept loss:** When you know how to lose and still avoid financial ruin, you will always preserve your wealth. What's more, dealing with loss is the most important trait of a long-term investor because it keeps you in the game.

3. **Compound your money:** Just sit back and let your money do the work. With enough time, your small investments grow into huge sums. Enjoy your life, and always remember that you're getting richer as long as you keep investing.

The beauty of this path is that it's available to each and every one of us. I'm the living proof of that. I came from a family that had nothing. I grew up in a small city. I was the only nonwhite kid in my class. And I could go on about my limitations for a while. I bet you could too. None of us have an easy life. After all, isn't that why you read this book?

You want to get wealthy. And you have the right to do so. You don't have to live from paycheck to paycheck, wondering what you will do if you ever lose your job. It's time to break free from that pattern. It's time to get rich.

Follow the path I've laid out here in this book. Trust me, it works. I wake up every day and don't ever think about money anymore. I simply do my work and fulfill my responsibilities with a smile on my face. I do this not because I'm extremely wealthy. I don't fear money because I trust myself. Stoicism helped me to cultivate strong habits that make me a better person and a better investor. I live by those habits every single day. That's why I have no financial stress. I could lose all my money tomorrow and I wouldn't fear for my future. I have the Stoic path to wealth, which will always lead me in the right direction.

As you're following the path, stay focused on your actions. Forget about the overnight success stories of million-dollar entrepreneurs on social media. Every day, your Stoic Edge becomes stronger. You will stay Stoic through recessions, pandemics, natural disasters, wars, and all the other chaos of life.

Nothing can stop you from investing. That's because you always have your mind on the real prize: freedom. That's why we ultimately do what we do. All of it. Investing in ourselves. Dealing with loss. Compounding our money in the market. None of it is fun. But it makes us mentally and financially stronger. And with that strength comes freedom.

I remember reading a blog post during the financial crisis of 2008, right after I lost a lot of money in the market. I don't know anymore where I read it or who wrote it. I just remember one sentence (which I'm paraphrasing): *If you own stocks and the thought of going through a recession doesn't send a shiver down your spine, then you're made of granite!*

This is why regular people fear stocks. They can't control the range of emotions they're going through when the market does what it does.

Well, we can. We're granite.

Happy investing.

Acknowledgments

Thank you, my reader. I always remind myself that without a reader there's no writer. Since 2015, readers have made me a writer. And I thank you for that.

Without the support of my mother, father, and brother, I would also not be a writer. With your consistent support and encouragement, particularly in the past eight years, I've built a solid writing career.

Everyone who directly contributed to *The Stoic Path*: THANK YOU. I always thought that writing was a solo pursuit. I was wrong. Writing a book is a true team effort. My research assistant, John Pucay, I appreciate your dedication and the energy you've put into supporting me with every chapter. You worked on this book like it was your own. My former assistant, Karl Balonzo, your early research in 2021 was excellent. To my agent, Julie Stevenson, who believed in this idea from the start and has been supporting me for more than two years of writing, our early conversations helped me to see the direction of the book. My editor, Merry Sun, helped me to improve my writing and take this book to the next level. Thank you to the rest of the editorial team for all your input, including Leila Sandlin. My publisher at Portfolio, Adrian Zackheim, and editor in chief, Niki Papadopoulos, thank you for taking this project on. The entire process has been so positive, energetic, and wonderful. You all gave this book fertile ground to grow. I'm grateful for that.

Thank you to Morgan Housel, Jimmy Soni, Tadas Viskanta, Scott Young, and Derek Sivers. I appreciate your support when I was still working on the book proposal.

The inspiration to write this book and its format were both influenced by the works of Robert Greene. He has influenced my thoughts on storytelling and sharing wisdom. He set a standard for nonfiction books like this one.

To be honest, I could go on for a while. There are so many people who've supported my writing over the past years. If we ever connected, I want you to know I deeply appreciate every atom of support I got. That's something my parents instilled in me. Growing up, we didn't have much but gratitude. Sharing your appreciation is free. But the effect it has on others is priceless. Thank you for spending this time with me. All the best.

Darius
June 2023

Notes

In this section you'll find a detailed list of references for each chapter in the book. I created these notes in a way that you can browse through them without continuously having to go back to the chapters. Every note starts with the sentence from the book that it corresponds to. My goal is to give credit to every person and resource I've used.

1. My Pursuit of Enduring Prosperity

6   **What's worse, not all wages:** Tami Luhby, "Wages Continue to Rise, but They Still Aren't Keeping Pace with Inflation," *CNN*, January 31, 2023, edition.cnn.com/2023/01/31/economy/workers -wages-fourth-quarter/index.html.

6   **Between 1980 and 2022, inflation:** "Value of $1 from 1980 to 2022," officialdata.org/us/inflation/1980?endYear=2022& amount=1.

6   **In comparison, the market:** "Stock Market Returns between 1980 and 2022," officialdata.org/us/stocks/s-p-500/1980 ?amount=1&endyear=2022.

6   **since the 1928 inception of the S&P 500:** J. B. Maverick, "S&P 500 Average Return," *Investopedia*, updated May 24, 2023, investopedia.com/ask/answers/042415/what-average-annual -return-sp-500.asp.

7 **Forty-two years later, in 2022:** The "real value" of a single U.S. dollar decreases over time. In other words, a dollar will pay for fewer items at the store. "Value of $1 from 1980 to 2022."

7 **But if you had invested:** Adjusted for inflation, the $105,244.24 *nominal* end value of the original $1,000 investment would have an inflation-adjusted return of $29,632.50. "Stock Market Returns between 1980 and 2022."

7 **We also went through:** World Health Organization, "WHO Coronavirus (COVID-19) Dashboard," covid19.who.int/?map Filter=deaths.

8 **For example, the wealthiest:** Juliana Menasce Horowitz, Ruth Igielnik, and Rakesh Kochhar, "Trends in Income and Wealth Inequality," *Pew Research Center,* January 9, 2020, pewresearch .org/social-trends/2020/01/09/trends-in-income-and-wealth-in equality.

8 **Data show that for the 99 percent:** Robert Frank, "Where the Rich Make Their Income," *CNBC,* April 9, 2015, cnbc.com /2015/04/09/where-the-rich-make-their-income.html.

9 **In 2011, individual investors:** BNY Mellon Wealth Management, "The Rise of Retail Traders," November 2021, bnymel lonwealth.com/insights/the-rise-of-retail-traders.html.

9 **In 2022, the frequency:** George Smith, "Is 2022 One of the Most Volatile Years Ever for Stocks?," *LPL Research,* September 1, 2022, lplresearch.com/2022/09/01/is-2022-one-of-the-most -volatile-years-ever-for-stocks.

10 **As I'm writing this:** World Federation of Exchanges, "Welcome to the Future of Markets," world-exchanges.org.

10 **Studies that look into the success:** Bob Pisani, "Attention Robinhood Power Users: Most Day Traders Lose Money," *CNBC,* November 20, 2020, cnbc.com/2020/11/20/attention-robinhood -power-users-most-day-traders-lose-money.html.

11 **About 80 percent of professional:** Josh Meyers, "New Report Finds Almost 80% of Active Fund Managers Are Falling Behind the Major Indexes," *CNBC,* March 27, 2022, cnbc.com/2022 /03/27/new-report-finds-almost-80percent-of-active-fund -managers-are-falling-behind.html.

11 **In the year 2021 alone:** Dean Talbot, "Business Book Sales Statistics," *WordsRated*, December 20, 2022, wordsrated.com /business-books-statistics.

12 **"Individuals who cannot master":** Andy Shuler, "9 Top Benjamin Graham Quotes on Value Investing," *eInvesting for Beginners*, November 21, 2019, einvestingforbeginners.com/benjamin -graham-quotes-ashul.

12 **I experienced that during:** John Carney, "America Lost $10.2 Trillion in 2008," *Business Insider*, February 3, 2009, businessin sider.com/2009/2/america-lost-102-trillion-of-wealth-in-2008 ?international=true&r=US&IR=T.

13 **"Every emotion is weak at first":** Lucius Annaeus Seneca, *Selected Letters*, trans. Elaine Fantham (Oxford: Oxford University Press, 2010), 253.

14 **My big test came:** Bob Pisani, "One Year Ago, Stocks Dropped 12% in a Single Day. What Investors Have Learned Since Then," *CNBC*, March 16, 2021, cnbc.com/2021/03/16/one -year-ago-stocks-dropped-12percent-in-a-single-day-what -investors-have-learned-since-then.html.

2. Build Wealth by Applying Ancient Wisdom

16 **Stoicism is a philosophical school:** Joshua J. Mark, "Zeno of Citium," *World History Encyclopedia*, February 15, 2011, world history.org/Zeno_of_Citium.

20 **"If you can make money":** Chuck Chakrapani, *The Good Life Handbook: Epictetus' Stoic Classic Enchiridion* (Toronto: Stoic Gym, 2016), 69.

3. How to Build a Stoic Edge in Three Steps

22 **Among its holdings are:** "Berkshire Hathaway: Everything You Need to Know," *Insurance Business*, accessed July 24, 2023, insurancebusinessmag.com/us/companies/berkshire-hathaway /117652.

23 **He has an information edge:** "How Warren Buffett Keeps Up with a Torrent of Information," *Farnam Street*, n.d., fs.blog /warren-buffett-information.

23 **It also happens that Buffett:** Bloomberg editors, "Buffett Nears a Milestone He Doesn't Want: $100 Billion in Cash," *Money*, August 7, 2017, money.com/warren-buffett-berkshire-hathaway -too-much-cash.

25 **A survey showed that half:** Stash Team, "90% of Americans Want to Invest but Almost Half Don't Know Where to Start," *Stash*, August 9, 2022, stash.com/learn/90-of-americans-want -to-invest-but-almost-half-dont-know-where-to-start.

26 **The S&P 500's return:** Caroline Banton, "The Rule of 72: What It Is and How to Use It in Investing," *Investopedia*, updated June 18, 2023, investopedia.com/ask/answers/what-is-the -rule-72.

29 **"That things have no hold on the soul":** Marcus Aurelius, *Meditations*, trans. Gregory Hays (New York: Modern Library, 2003), 36.

Principle One: Invest In Yourself

31 **"Not to assume it's impossible":** Marcus Aurelius, *Meditations*, trans. Gregory Hays (New York: Modern Library, 2003), 73.

4. Valuable Skills Are Better Than Money

33 **Today, Livermore is considered:** Lucinda Shen, "Why Wall Street Traders Are Obsessed with Jesse Livermore," *Business Insider*, July 17, 2015, businessinsider.com/the-life-of-jesse-livermore -2015-7.

34 **He hated the idea:** Tom Rubython, *Jesse Livermore: Boy Plunger; The Man Who Sold America Short in 1929* (Northamptonshire, UK: Myrtle Press, 2014).

34 **When he arrived in 1891:** Rubython, *Jesse Livermore*.

34 **He simply wrote down:** Rubython, *Jesse Livermore*.

34 **To his surprise, Livermore discovered:** Rubython, *Jesse Livermore.*

35 **Livermore, determined to keep trading:** Rubython, *Jesse Livermore.*

36 **At one point, the size:** David Hochfelder, "'Where the Common People Could Speculate': The Ticker, Bucket Shops, and the Origins of Popular Participation in Financial Markets, 1880–1920," *Journal of American History* 93, no. 2 (September 1, 2006): 335–58, doi.org/10.2307/4486233.

36 **Because bucket shops were also used:** From 1897, authorities started to close bucket shops in New York. They closed the last one there in 1908. "Big Raid on Bucket Shops," *New York Times*, April 24, 1897, nytimes.com/1897/04/24/archives/big-raid-on -bucket-shops-three-new-street-houses-closed-in-the.html.

36 **In one of his most memorable:** Rubython, *Jesse Livermore.*

36 **In 1907 he began:** Edwin Lefevre, *Reminiscences of a Stock Operator* (New York: George H. Doran, 1923).

37 **In mid-October, the New York Stock Exchange:** Ellen Terrell, "United Copper, Wall Street, and the Panic of 1907," *Inside Adams* (blog), Library of Congress, March 9, 2021, blogs.loc.gov /inside_adams/2021/03/united-copper-panic-of-1907.

37 **He lost his entire fortune:** Shen, "Why Wall Street Traders Are Obsessed."

37 **"I don't have to beat Wall Street":** Richard Smitten, *Jesse Livermore: World's Greatest Stock Trader* (New York: John Wiley & Sons, 2001), 36.

38 **In two days, billions of dollars:** ET Bureau, "Market Crash of 1929: Some Facts of the Economic Downturn," *Economic Times*, October 22, 2017, economictimes.indiatimes.com/industry/mis cellaneous/market-crash-of-1929-some-facts-of-the-economic -downturn/articleshow/61166918.cms?from=mdr.

39 **"the goal of life":** Ryan Holiday and Stephen Hanselman, *Lives of the Stoics: The Art of Living from Zeno to Marcus Aurelius* (New York: Portfolio/Penguin, 2020), 27.

39 **"The future belongs to those":** Robert Greene, *Mastery* (New York: Viking Adult, 2012), 80.

40   **"What then is education?":** Epictetus, *Enchiridion (with a Selection from the Discourses)*, trans. George Long (Overland Park, KS: Digireads.com, 2016), 71.

41   **"search yourself and examine":** Lucius Annaeus Seneca, *Selected Letters*, trans. Elaine Fantham (Oxford: Oxford University Press, 2010), 31.

42   **"Mastery of reading and writing":** Marcus Aurelius, *Meditations*, trans. Gregory Hays (New York: Modern Library, 2003), 156.

43   **"Now is the time to get serious":** Epictetus, *The Art of Living: The Classical Manual on Virtue, Happiness, and Effectiveness*, trans. Sharon Lebell (San Francisco: Harper Collins, 1995), 90.

43   **"You're not yet Socrates":** Epictetus, *Discourses and Selected Writings*, trans. Robert Dobbin (New York: Penguin Classics, 2008), 255.

43   **"Writing is learned by imitation":** William Zinsser, "Looking for a Model," *American Scholar*, December 2, 2011, theamericanscholar.org/looking-for-a-model/#.VVSw70JYzA4.

45   **"Only the educated are free":** Epictetus, *Discourses: Books 1 and 2*, trans. P. E. Matheson (Mineola, NY: Dover Publications, 2004), 144.

5. The Hidden Principles of the Market

48   **In the spring of 1950:** Roger Lowenstein, *Buffett: The Making of an American Capitalist* (New York: Random House, 1995).

49   **"I looked about sixteen":** Kathleen Elkins, "22 Mind-Blowing Facts about Warren Buffett and His Wealth," *Business Insider*, September 23, 2015, businessinsider.com/facts-about-warren-buffett-2015-9.

49   **In fact, from the creation:** Alice Schroeder, *The Snowball: Warren Buffett and the Business of Life* (New York: Bantam Books, 2008).

49   **That strategy of buying and selling:** Brian Domitrovic, "Why Did People Buy Stocks in the 1920s?," *Forbes*, January 9, 2020, forbes.com/sites/briandomitrovic/2020/01/09/why-did-people-buy-stocks-in-the-1920s.

49   **People bought stocks at high prices:** Domitrovic, "Why Did People Buy Stocks?"

49   **Looking further back:** Edgar Lawrence Smith, *Common Stocks as Long Term Investments* (New York: Macmillan, 1924).

51   **Buffett famously:** Joshua Kennon, "How Did Warren Buffett Become So Rich?" *The Balance,* updated July 5, 2022, thebalance money.com/warren-buffett-timeline-356439.

51   **"I was twenty-one":** Schroeder, *Snowball,* 131.

51   **"My service station was the dumbest":** Schroeder, *Snowball,* 129.

52   **"I was the only one":** Schroeder, *Snowball,* 151.

54   **stock markets really started:** Mark Casson and John S. Lee, "The Origin and Development of Markets: A Business History Perspective," *Business History Review* 85, no. 1 (May 11, 2011): 9–37, doi.org/10.1017/S0007680511000018.

54   **For example, transactions between:** Charles M. Jones, "Century of Stock Market Liquidity and Trading Costs," Columbia Business School Research Paper Series, May 22, 2002, www0 .gsb.columbia.edu/mygsb/faculty/research/pubfiles/4048/A %20century%20of%20Market%20Liquidity%20and%20Trading %20Costs.pdf.

56   **In the 1920s, investors assumed:** "General Electric Co. History, Profile and Corporate Video," Companies History, accessed July 26, 2023, companieshistory.com/general-electric.

60   **"In business, financial and market cycles":** Howard Marks, *Mastering the Market Cycle: Getting the Odds on Your Side* (Boston: Houghton Mifflin Harcourt, 2018), 93.

62   **"When jarred, unavoidably":** Marcus Aurelius, *Meditations,* trans. Gregory Hays (New York: Modern Library, 2003), 70.

62   **"Buy American. I Am":** Warren E. Buffett, "Buy American. I Am," *New York Times,* October 16, 2008, nytimes.com/2008/10 /17/opinion/17buffett.html.

62   **"Make progress":** Lucius Annaeus *Seneca, Seneca's Letters from a Stoic,* trans. Richard Mott Gummere (Mineola, NY: Dover Publications, 2016), 84.

6. Consistency Pays Off: Investing Is a Habit

65 **More than a decade after it started:** Robert D. Hershey Jr., "Geraldine Weiss Dies at 96; Blazed a Trail for Women in Investing," *New York Times*, April 26, 2022, nytimes.com/2022/04 /26/business/geraldine-weiss-dead.html.

66 **When Weiss appeared:** Kevin LeVick, "Geraldine Weiss: 'The Grande Dame of Dividends,'" *The Street*, March 23, 2021, thestreet.com/dictionary/geraldine-weiss-the-grand-dame-of -dividends.

66 **Weiss decided to use a pseudonym:** "Geraldine Weiss," Capitol Private Wealth Group, n.d., capitolpwg.com/wp-content /uploads/2017/07/Geraldine-Weiss.pdf.

66 **Yale and Princeton:** Katie McLaughlin, "5 Things Women Couldn't Do in the 1960s," *CNN*, August 25, 2014, edition.cnn .com/2014/08/07/living/sixties-women-5-things/index.html.

66 **Weiss remembered running:** Shenandoah Weiss, "Geraldine Weiss Levine Interviewed by Granddaughters in 2011," January 21, 2012, YouTube video, 56:31, youtu.be/ep-_MRu45Wc.

67 **"After all of my reading":** "Dividend Stocks Pay Off," *Forbes*, February 12, 2002, forbes.com/2002/02/12/0212adviser.html? sh=31a7d6163dbd.

67 **As Weiss said, "the goal":** Weiss, "Geraldine Weiss Levine Interviewed."

67 **"We were living hand to mouth":** Amanda Leek, "How to Invest Like . . . Geraldine Weiss, the Queen of Blue-Chip Dividends," *Telegraph*, September 18, 2017, telegraph.co.uk/money /special-reports/invest-likegeraldine-weissthe-queen-blue-chip -dividends.

68 **"Never is there a better time":** Anupam Nagar, "Geraldine Weiss' Mantra for Investing Success: Stay with High Dividend–Paying Stocks," *Economic Times*, February 20, 2021, economic times.indiatimes.com/markets/stocks/news/bluechip-stocks -guru-geraldine-weiss-success-mantra-bet-on-high-dividend -paying-companies/articleshow/81124897.cms.

69 **"I will never forget":** Geraldine Weiss, "Happy Birthday, I.Q. Trends," *IQ Trends*, April 1, 2006, tayloredge.com/bits-n -pieces/news/happybirthday.pdf.

69 **Between 1986 and 2022, its recommendations:** Hershey Jr., "Geraldine Weiss Dies at 96."

70 **"Every habit and faculty":** Epictetus, *Enchiridion (with a Selection from the Discourses)*, trans. George Long (Overland Park, KS: Digireads.com, 2016), 120.

71 **"How then would knowing":** *Musonius Rufus: Lectures and Sayings*, trans. Cynthia King (North Charleston, SC: CreateSpace, 2011), 34.

72 **"Suppose you like a ceramic cup":** Chuck Chakrapani, *The Good Life Handbook: Epictetus' Stoic Classic Enchiridion* (Toronto: The Stoic Gym, 2016), 69.

75 **"For there is no other reason":** *Musonius Rufus*, 38.

76 **"It does not make much difference":** Lucius Annaeus Seneca, *Selected Letters*, trans. Elaine Fantham (Oxford: Oxford University Press, 2010), 115.

Principle Two: Accept Loss

79 **"If you want to improve":** Epictetus, "The *Enchiridion*, Translated by Elizabeth Carter," The Internet Classics Archive, accessed July 24, 2023, classics.mit.edu/Epictetus/epicench.html.

7. Get Comfortable with Short-Term Losses

81 **"I was very fearful":** FINAiUS, "How Cathie Wood Became the Queen of Retail Investors," November 20, 2021, YouTube video, 30:12, youtu.be/CIXH1cceujg.

82 **"The focus on such a long-term":** Adam Shell, "ARK Invest's Cathie Wood Reveals Her Successful Playbook," *Investor's Business Daily*, October 29, 2020, investors.com/news/manage ment/leaders-and-success/cathie-wood-ark-invest-shows-you -her-winning-playbook.

83 **Tupelo had roughly $1.3 billion:** "Tupelo Capital Management, L.L.C., 13F Report for Period Ending 2000-03-31," United States Securities and Exchange Commission, accessed on July 26, 2023, sec.gov/Archives/edgar/data/1080349/000095012300004921/0000950123-00-004921.txt.

83 **Tupelo's total AUM had fallen to around $200 million:** "Tupelo Capital Management, L.L.C."

83 **She pitched her idea:** Michael Wursthorn, "Cathie Wood, Meme-Stock Champion Who Bet Big on Tesla and Bitcoin, Stands Her Ground," *Wall Street Journal*, August 6, 2021, wsj.com/articles/cathie-wood-ark-guiding-light-meme-stock-investing-11628258307.

84 **According to an analysis:** Rebecca Lake, "History of IPOs That Failed," *SoFi*, March 8, 2022, sofi.com/learn/content/ipos-that-failed/#.

84 **When Wood started ARK:** Matt Phillips, "God, Money, YOLO: How Cathie Wood Found Her Flock," *New York Times*, August 22, 2021, nytimes.com/2021/08/22/business/cathie-wood-ark-stocks.html.

84 **In 2016, two years after:** "ARK Innovation ETF ARKK: Performance," Morningstar, morningstar.com/etfs/arcx/arkk/performance.

84 **She even signed an agreement:** Claire Ballentine, "Cathie Wood's Ark Invest Rocked as Shareholder Seeks Control," *Bloomberg*, November 16, 2020, bloomberg.com/news/articles/2020-11-16/takeover-battle-emerges-for-cathie-wood-s-ark-in-stellar-year.

85 **By the end of 2016:** Hayley C. Cuccinello, "'Go For It': America's Richest Self-Made Women on Founding Businesses after 40," *Forbes*, October 13, 2020, forbes.com/sites/hayleycuccinello/2020/10/13/american-self-made-women-founders-over-40.

85 **The following year, in 2017:** "ARK Innovation ETF (ARKK) Performance," *Yahoo! Finance*, finance.yahoo.com/quote/ARKK/performance.

85 **By early 2021, ARK had:** Claire Ballentine, "Cathie Wood Amasses $50 Billion and a New Nickname: 'Money Tree,'"

Bloomberg, February 5, 2021, bloomberg.com/news/articles /2021-02-05/cathie-wood-amasses-50-billion-and-a-new -nickname-money-tree.

85 **But though her main fund:** Jack Pitcher, "Investors Are Losing Faith in Cathie Wood's ARK Innovation," *Wall Street Journal*, December 12, 2022, wsj.com/articles/investors-are-losing-faith -in-cathie-woods-ark-innovation-11670846139.

85 **In a December 2022 tweet:** Cathie Wood (@CathieDWood), "The financial world criticizes and denigrates @ARKInvest's research and investment focus on exponential growth: it dismisses our forecasts of the massive latent profitability in companies sacrificing short-term profitability for exponential and highly profitable long term growth," Twitter, December 4, 2022, 10:53 a.m. ET, twitter.com/CathieDWood/status/1599431785431326721.

86 **In 2018, Tesla's stock price:** Grace Dean, "Elon Musk Says Tesla Was Just a Month Away from Bankruptcy While It Ramped Up Production of the Model 3," *Business Insider*, November 4, 2020, businessinsider.com/elon-musk-tesla-bankruptcy-model-3 -electric-vehicle-ev-production-2020-11.

86 **Tesla traded at around $22:** "Tesla Stock Price in 2018," StatMuse, statmuse.com/money/ask/tesla+stock+price+in+ 2018#.

86 **But Wood boldly stated:** In 2018, Wood predicted Tesla would hit $4,000. That price was before the five-to-one and three-to-one stock splits. Adjusted for the splits, her prediction was roughly $260. Matthew J. Belvedere, "Tesla Stock Going to $4,000—That Would be an Increase of 1,100%: Money Manager Catherine Wood," *CNBC*, February 7, 2018, cnbc.com /2018/02/07/ark-chief-catherine-wood-sees-tesla-stock-going -to-4000.html.

86 **A year later, Tesla stock:** Tesla traded at around $300 when Wood made her prediction in 2018. The stock reached a low of $177 in June 2019. These prices are before the stock splits. Alan Farley, "Slumping Tesla Stock Headed into Test of 2019 Low," *Investopedia*, August 15, 2019, investopedia.com/slumping-tesla -stock-headed-into-test-of-2019-low-4767681.

86   **But in January 2021:** Matthew Fox, "ARK's Cathie Wood Made a Monster Call in 2018 That Tesla Stock Would Hit $4,000. Her Prediction Just Came True 2 Years Early," *Business Insider,* January 8, 2021, markets.businessinsider.com/news/stocks /tesla-stock-analysis-cathie-wood-ark-prediction-just-came-true -2021-1-1029944356.

87   **"He never exhibited rudeness":** Marcus Aurelius, *Meditations,* trans. Gregory Hays (New York: Modern Library, 2003), 10.

89   **"My baker has no bread":** Lucius Annaeus Seneca, *Selected Letters,* trans. Elaine Fantham (Oxford: Oxford University Press, 2010), 267.

89   **In the history of the S&P:** "Percentage Positive and Negative Days across Various Periods: S&P 500 Index," Crestmont Research, n.d., crestmontresearch.com/docs/Stock-Yo-Yo.pdf.

91   **For example, in early 2023:** Ben Ward, "Cathie Wood's Been Busy Adding to ARK Invest's Holdings, Buying Tesla, Coinbase and More," *Nasdaq,* April 20, 2023, nasdaq.com/articles/cathie -woods-been-busy-adding-to-ark-invests-holdings-buying-tesla -coinbase-and-more.

92   **"The soul is strengthened":** *Musonius Rufus, Lectures and Sayings,* trans. Cynthia King (North Charleston, SC: CreateSpace, 2011), 37.

8. Avoid Losing All Your Money

95   **Thorp, born in 1932:** Edward O. Thorp, *A Man for All Markets: From Las Vegas to Wall Street, How I Beat the Dealer and the Market* (New York: Random House, 2017).

96   **When he boldly shared:** Jacob Goldstein, "Episode 749: Professor Blackjack," January 20, 2017, in *Planet Money,* podcast transcript, npr.org/transcripts/510810752.

96   **Thorp pocketed $11,000 on that trip:** Robert Blincoe, "Defining Moment: A Professor Temporarily Turns the Tables on the Casinos, 1962," *Financial Times,* November 28, 2009, ft.com/content/99075802-d7de-11de-b578-00144feabdc0.

97   **"This plan, of betting only":** Thorp, *Man for All Markets*, 88.

97   **"greatest gambling arena on earth":** Thorp, *Man for All Markets*, 144.

97   **In 1969, Thorp quit:** Burton G. Malkiel, "The Math Whiz and the Money," *Wall Street Journal*, January 29, 2017, wsj.com /articles/the-math-whiz-and-the-money-1485733245.

97   **Thorp simply recouped his money:** "Stock Market Returns between 1969 and 1973," officialdata.org/us/stocks/s-p -500/1969?amount=100&endYear=1973.

98   **"What were my mistakes?":** Thorp, *Man for All Markets*, 146.

98   **By 1975, six years after:** Michael Hiltzik, "Beating the Odds: Ed Thorp Tells How He Invented Card Counting and Made a Fortune on Wall Street," *Los Angeles Times*, February 17, 2017, latimes.com/business/hiltzik/la-fi-hiltzik-thorp-20170217-story .html.

98   **He observed that there were people:** Thorp, *Man for All Markets*, 177–78.

98   **The fund boasted sixteen general partners:** Roger Lowenstein, *When Genius Failed: The Rise and Fall of Long-Term Capital Management* (New York: Random House, 2000), 67–77.

99   **"Meriwether had a history at Salomon":** Thorp, *Man for All Markets*, 265.

99   **pompously started another hedge fund:** Sam Jones, "Meriwether's JWM Partners Winds Down Flagship Fund," *Financial Times*, July 8, 2009, ft.com/content/21a6bbee-6c00-11de -9320-00144feabdc0.

100   **never had a losing year:** Scott Patterson, "Old Pros Size Up the Game," *Wall Street Journal*, March 22, 2008, wsj.com/articles /SB120614130030156085.

100   **"Success on Wall Street was getting":** Thorp, *Man for All Markets*, 213.

101   **"No one ever suddenly became depraved":** *Encyclopaedia Britannica*, s.v. "Juvenal: Quotes," britannica.com/quotes/Juvenal.

103   **The majority of these newly listed:** Corrie Driebusch, "IPO Stocks Have Tumbled, Hobbling Demand for New Listings," *Wall Street Journal*, September 26, 2022, wsj.com/articles

/poor-ipo-stock-performance-weighs-further-on-new-issue
-market-11664184781.

103   **"Markets can remain irrational":** It's not clear whether
Keynes truly said this. "The Market Can Remain Irrational
Longer Than You Can Remain Solvent," *Quote Investigator*, n.d.,
quoteinvestigator.com/2011/08/09/remain-solvent.

104   **"Characteristics of the rational soul":** Marcus Aurelius,
Meditations, trans. Gregory Hays (New York: Modern Library,
2003), 147.

105   **"For freedom is not procured":** Epictetus, *The Works of
Epictetus: His Discourses, in Four Books, the Enchiridion, and Fragments*,
trans. Thomas Wentworth Higginson (New York: Thomas Nel-
son and Sons, 1890), 2149.

106   **Since 1926, the U.S. stock market:** Ben Carlson, "The
Stock Market Is Not a Casino," *A Wealth of Common Sense* (blog),
May 25, 2023, awealthofcommonsense.com/2023/05/the-stock
-market-is-not-a-casino.

107   **As Marcus Aurelius said, we must:** Aurelius, *Meditations*, 106.

108   **"A healthy mind should be prepared":** Aurelius, *Meditations*, 142.

9. Greed Is Not Good

111   **When Morgan launched the Wellington Fund:** "VWELX
Vanguard Wellington Fund Investor Shares," Vanguard, investor
.vanguard.com/investment-products/mutual-funds/profile
/VWELX.

111   **The sixty-six-year-old Morgan:** John C. Bogle, *Stay the
Course: The Story of Vanguard and the Index Revolution* (Hoboken, NJ:
Wiley, 2018).

111   **The term "go-go":** James Chen, "Go-Go Fund," *Investopedia*,
June 30, 2022, investopedia.com/terms/g/go-go-fund.asp.

111   **He studied economics at Princeton:** Edward Wyatt, "John
C. Bogle, Founder of Financial Giant Vanguard, Is Dead at 89,"
New York Times, January 16, 2019, nytimes.com/2019/01/16
/obituaries/john-bogle-vanguard-dead.html.

111   **Bogle started working at Wellington:** Kathleen Elkins, "Jack Bogle Shares the $1 Billion Investing Mistake That Cost Him His Job," *CNBC*, December 21, 2018, cnbc.com/2018/12/20/jack-bogles-biggest-investing-mistake-cost-1-billion-and-his-job.html.

111   **became Wellington's CEO in 1970:** Rick Ferri, "What Was John Bogle Thinking?" *Forbes*, February 10, 2014, forbes.com/sites/rickferri/2014/02/10/what-was-john-bogle-thinking/?sh=ac281be68e71.

111   **Bogle was fired in 1974:** Elkins, "Jack Bogle Shares."

112   **Though Bogle had gone along:** Bogle, *Stay the Course.*

112   **In fact, in his 1951 Princeton:** John Clifton Bogle, "The Economic Role of the Investment Company" (senior thesis, Princeton University, 1951), available at dataspace.princeton.edu/handle/88435/dsp017m01bm63k.

112   **While he always liked the idea:** Jason Zweig, "Birth of the Index Mutual Fund: 'Bogle's Folly' Turns 40," *Jason Zweig* (blog), August 31, 2016, jasonzweig.com/birth-of-the-index-mutual-fund-bogles-folly-turns-40.

112   **In the beginning, the company:** Laura Southwick, "Jack and the Bogleheads: How Vanguard Changed Investing Forever," *Juno Finance* (blog), March 4, 2021, juno.finance/blog/John-bogle-bogleheads-vanguard-history.

113   **"I can't believe that the great":** John C. Bogle, "Bogle Sounds a Warning on Index Funds," *Wall Street Journal*, November 29, 2018, wsj.com/articles/bogle-sounds-a-warning-on-index-funds-1543504551.

113   **People were already calling:** Jason Zweig, "Birth of the Index Mutual Fund: 'Bogle's Folly' Turns 40," *Wall Street Journal*, updated August 31, 2016, wsj.com/articles/BL-MBB-52953.

113   **To many people on Wall Street:** "Jack Bogle: The Man Who Pioneered Index Investing," *BBC News*, January 17, 2019, bbc.com/news/business-46906246.

113   **"While all of our peers":** John C. Bogle, "How the Index Fund Was Born," *Wall Street Journal*, September 3, 2011, wsj.com/articles/SB10001424053111904583204576544681577401622.

113 **While Vanguard started:** CNBC.com staff, "Jack Bogle, Index Mutual Fund Pioneer," *CNBC*, April 29, 2014, cnbc.com/2014 /04/29/25-jack-bogle.html.

113 **Six years later, Vanguard hit:** Bogle, *Stay the Course*.

113 **$8.1 *trillion* in assets:** "Assets Under Management (AUM) of Vanguard in 1975, 1990, 2005 and 2022 (in Billion U.S. Dollars)," *Statista*, accessed July 28, 2023, statista.com/statistics /1260855/vanguard-aum.

114 **second-largest asset manager in America:** "Largest Asset Managers Worldwide as of March 2022, by Value of Managed Assets (in Trillion U.S. Dollars)," *Statista*, accessed July 28, 2023, statista.com/statistics/322452/largest-asset-managers-world wide-by-value-of-assets.

114 **When he died at age eighty-nine:** Shawn M. Carter, "This Was Jack Bogle's 'Only Regret about Money,'" *CNBC*, January 18, 2019, cnbc.com/2019/01/18/jack-bogles-only-money-regret .html.

114 **$12.2 billion in the same year:** Nir Kaissar, "He Should Be a Billionaire, but Jack Bogle Chose to Make Others Richer," *Sydney Morning Herald*, January 19, 2019, smh.com.au/business /markets/he-should-be-a-billionaire-but-jack-bogle-chose-to -make-others-richer-20190119-p50sd8.html.

114 **Bogle regularly gave half:** Wyatt, "John C. Bogle, Founder of Financial Giant."

114 **If he and his heirs had been:** Jeff Sommer, "Vanguard's Jack Bogle Wasn't a Billionaire. He Was Proud of That.," *New York Times*, January 16, 2019, nytimes.com/2019/01/16/business /vanguard-jack-bogle-death.html.

114 **"How much money is enough":** *New World Encyclopedia*, s.v. "John D. Rockefeller," newworldencyclopedia.org/entry/John _D._Rockefeller.

114 **"$1 more than you need":** John C. Bogle, *Enough: True Measures of Money, Business, and Life* (Hoboken, NJ: Wiley, 2008), 239.

114 **From the beginning, the Stoics:** For a detailed discussion of the commonalities and differences among Stoicism, Epicureanism, and Cynicism, watch this lecture by Professor Edith Hall.

She is a British scholar of classics, specializing in ancient Greek literature and cultural history: Edith Hall, "Cynics, Stoics, Epicureans," Gresham College, May 27, 2021, video, 45:58, gresham .ac.uk/watch-now/cynics-stoics-epicureans.

115 **"proper measure of wealth?":** Lucius Annaeus Seneca, *Selected Letters*, trans. Elaine Fantham (Oxford: Oxford University Press, 2010), 5.

115 **When the post-COVID stock market:** Ethan Wolff-Mann, "43% of Retail Investors Are Trading with Leverage: Survey," *Yahoo! Finance*, September 9, 2020, finance.yahoo.com/news/43-of -retail-investors-are-trading-with-leverage-survey-172744302.html.

116 **"Could someone acquire instant":** *Musonius Rufus: Lectures and Sayings*, trans. Cynthia King (North Charleston, SC: CreateSpace, 2011), 36.

117 **"If you desire something outside":** Chuck Chakrapani, *The Good Life Handbook: Epictetus' Stoic Classic Enchiridion* (Toronto: Stoic Gym, 2016), 69.

118 **"choice and refusal":** William B. Irvine, *A Guide to the Good Life: The Ancient Art of Stoic Joy* (Oxford: Oxford University Press, 2008), 54.

119 **"The person who eats more":** *Musonius Rufus*, 74.

121 **"Is it not madness":** Irvine, *A Guide to the Good Life*, 173.

Principle Three: Compound Your Money

123 **"Moral recommendations behave like seeds":** Lucius Annaeus Seneca, *Selected Letters*, trans. Elaine Fantham (Oxford: Oxford University Press, 2010), 60.

10. Let Your Money Do the Work

125 **Peter Lynch was just ten:** Peter Lynch and John Rothchild, *One Up on Wall Street: How to Use What You Already Know to Make Money in the Market* (New York: Penguin Books, 1989).

126 **Sullivan and other executives:** Anne Fisher, "From Golf Caddy to Big Shot: No Accidental Path," *Fortune*, July 17, 2013,

fortune.com/2013/07/17/from-golf-caddy-to-big-shot-no
-accidental-path.

126   **He used his stock market profits:** "Betting on the Market
Pros: Peter Lynch," PBS, n.d., pbs.org/wgbh/pages/frontline
/shows/betting/pros/lynch.html.

126   **That internship turned into:** "Peter Lynch Resource Page,"
Value Walk, n.d., valuewalk.com/peter-lynch-resource-page.

127   **He achieved a 20 percent return:** Peter Lynch and John
Rothchild, *Beating the Street* (New York: Simon & Schuster, 1992).

127   **In June 1982, Lynch said:** Lynch and Rothchild, *Beating the
Street*, 149.

128   **Chrysler was at $2 a share in 1982:** Lynch and Rothchild,
Beating the Street, 148.

128   **This meant he had to work:** Anise C. Wallace, "Mutual Fund
Champion Quits as Magellan Head," *New York Times*, March 29,
1990, nytimes.com/1990/03/29/business/mutual-fund-champion
-quits-as-magellan-head.html.

128   **The S&P 500 declined 20.4 percent:** Ryan McKeon and Jef-
frey M. Netter, "What Caused the 1987 Stock Market Crash and
Lessons for the 2008 Crash," *Review of Accounting and Finance* 8, no.
2 (January 19, 2009): 123–37, dx.doi.org/10.2139/ssrn.1330220.

128   **"Whether it's a 508-point day":** Lynch and Rothchild, *One
Up on Wall Street*, 36.

129   **He had grown the fund:** Steven Perlberg, "Mutual Fund
Legend Peter Lynch Identifies His 'Three C's' of Investing in a
Rare Interview," *Business Insider*, December 6, 2013, business
insider.com/peter-lynch-charlie-rose-investing-2013-12.

129   **"It wasn't the pressure":** "Betting on the Market Pros: Peter
Lynch."

131   **"Everyone approaches with more courage":** Lucius Annaeus Seneca, *Selected Letters*, trans. Elaine Fantham (Oxford:
Oxford University Press, 2010), 228.

131   **"Let no one rob me":** Lucius Annaeus Seneca, *On the Shortness of Life: Life Is Long if You Know How to Use It*, trans. C. D. N.
Costa (London: Penguin Books, 2005), 68.

132 **Albert Einstein called compounding:** Maurie Backman, "Einstein Said Compound Interest Is the 8th Wonder of the World. Why Graham Stephan Thinks That's Right," *The Ascent,* January 5, 2023, fool.com/the-ascent/buying-stocks/articles/einstein -said-compound-interest-is-the-8th-wonder-of-the-world-why -graham-stephan-thinks-thats-right.

132 **"Stop the excuses":** Epictetus, *The Art of Living: The Classical Manual on Virtue, Happiness, and Effectiveness,* trans. Sharon Lebell (San Francisco: Harper Collins, 1995), 90.

133 **In Epictetus's words, you must:** Epictetus, *The Art of Living,* 90.

135 **"Given that all must die":** *Musonius Rufus: Lectures and Sayings,* trans. Cynthia King (North Charleston, SC: CreateSpace, 2011), 86.

11. Trust Your Judgment

137 **He briefly pursued a PhD:** Julia La Roche, "The Fabulous Life of Stanley Druckenmiller—the Hedge Funder Who Says Old People Are Robbing Young People Blind," *Business Insider,* March 5, 2013, businessinsider.com/life-of-stanley-druckenmiller -2013-3.

138 **Within just three months:** Sebastian Mallaby, *More Money Than God: Hedge Funds and the Making of a New Elite* (New York: Penguin Press, 2010).

138 **Eventually, Druckenmiller's success:** "The Saturday Story: Soros Loses $2 Billion," *Independent,* November 1, 1997, inde pendent.co.uk/life-style/the-saturday-story-soros-loses-2-billion -1291410.html.

138 **Soros had started his own fund:** George Soros, *Soros on Soros: Staying Ahead of the Curve* (New York: John Wiley & Sons, 1995), 47; "Outwitting the Markets: 1969–80," Soros Fund Management LLC, Encyclopedia.com, accessed July 26, 2023, encyclo pedia.com/books/politics-and-business-magazines/soros-fund -management-llc#:~:text=in%20capital%2C%20including-, %24250%2C000,-of%20his%20own.

138 **A typical fund in the seventies:** In 1968, the SEC counted 140 investment partnerships as hedge funds. By the end of 1970, the biggest twenty-eight funds had declined by 70 percent. The total value of remaining funds at the time was $300 million. Alan Rappeport, "A Short History of Hedge Funds," *CFO*, March 27, 2007, cfo.com/banking-capital-markets/2007/03/a-short-history -of-hedge-funds.

138 **When Soros reached out:** Mallaby, *More Money Than God.*

138 **Druckenmiller asked his mentors:** Jack D. Schwager, *The New Market Wizards: Conversations with America's Top Traders* (New York: HarperCollins, 1992).

138 **From the start, he was:** Schwager, *New Market Wizards*, 262.

139 **"Even being coached":** Schwager, *New Market Wizards*, 262.

139 **Druckenmiller ended up:** Soros, *Soros on Soros*, 61.

139 **Things came to a head:** Katherine Burton, "Druckenmiller to Shut Fund after 30 Years as Stress Takes Toll," *Bloomberg*, August 19, 2010, bloomberg.com/news/articles/2010-08-18/drucken miller-calls-it-quits-after-30-years-as-hedge-fund-job-gets-tougher.

139 **"I want to leave,"** Mallaby, *More Money Than God*, 188.

139 **The following year, Druckenmiller grew:** Mallaby, *More Money Than God.*

139 **"It turned out to be a wonderful":** Soros, *Soros on Soros*, 62.

140 **On September 16, 1992:** Andrew Beattie, "How Did George Soros Break the Bank of England?" *Investopedia*, November 14, 2022, investopedia.com/ask/answers/08/george-soros-bank-of -england.asp.

140 **Because Soros loved the limelight:** Mallaby, *More Money Than God*, 208.

140 **Tech stocks behaved differently:** Gregory Zuckerman, "How the Soros Funds Lost Game of Chicken against Tech Stocks," *Wall Street Journal*, May 22, 2000, wsj.com/articles/SB95894419 575853588.

141 **Quantum Fund was down:** Michael Batnick, *Big Mistakes: The Best Investors and Their Worst Investments* (New York: Bloomberg Press, 2018).

142 **"What do you mean":** Zuckerman, "How the Soros Funds Lost."

142 **"I don't like this market":** Zuckerman, "How the Soros Funds Lost."

143 **"The idea of caring":** Anupam Nagar, "Tendencies Charlie Munger Wants You to Beat to Make Money in Market," *Economic Times*, November 7, 2020, economictimes.indiatimes.com/mar kets/stocks/news/tendencies-charlie-munger-wants-you-to-beat -to-make-money-in-market/articleshow/79097287.cms.

143 **"It would have been nice":** Floyd Norris, "Another Technol- ogy Victim? Top Soros Fund Manager Says He 'Overplayed' Hand," *New York Times*, April 29, 2000, nytimes.com/2000/04 /29/business/another-technology-victim-top-soros-fund-manager -says-he-overplayed-hand.html.

144 **"Choose not to be harmed":** Marcus Aurelius, *Meditations*, trans. Gregory Hays (New York: Modern Library, 2003), 39.

145 **This is what happened:** For a good analysis of the rotation from blockchain/crypto to AI, see Wright's Research, "Nvidia: Goodbye Crypto, Hello AI," *Seeking Alpha*, November 22, 2022, seekingalpha.com/article/4559930-nvidia-nvda-stock-goodbye -crypto-hello-ai.

145 **But many investors failed:** Desperate for profits, many companies within the blockchain and crypto industry tried to change their business models. Stacy Elliott, "Bitcoin Miners Are Pivoting in Search of Profits—and Hedging Their Bets," *Decrypt*, October 18, 2022, decrypt.co/112312/bitcoin-miners-pivoting -profits-hedging.

146 **"It is tragic for the soul":** Lucius Annaeus Seneca, *Seneca's Letters from a Stoic*, trans. Richard Mott Gummere (Mineola, NY: Dover Publications, 2016), 351–52.

146 **With his own fund:** Andrew Ross Sorkin and Peter Lattman, "Founder Terminating Hedge Fund," *New York Times*, August 18, 2010, nytimes.com/2010/08/19/business/19hedge.html.

147 **His $20 million investment:** Peter Elstrom, Pavel Alpeyev, and Lulu Yilun Chen, "Inside the Eccentric, Relentless Deal Making of SoftBank's Masayoshi Son," *Los Angeles Times*, Janu- ary 2, 2018, latimes.com/business/la-fi-tn-masayoshi-son-soft bank-20180102-story.html.

147 **"I was looking at the price":** Masayoshi Son, "Masayoshi Son Talks about Learning from Mistakes and Turning Them into Success | DealBook," *New York Times Events,* November 17, 2020, YouTube video, 48:41, youtube.com/watch?v=4KZrOf0lyUA.

148 **"People try to get away from it all":** Marcus Aurelius, *Meditations,* trans. Gregory Hays (New York: Modern Library, 2003), 37.

12. Stick to Your Investing Strategy

150 **His father, Om Pabrai:** William Green, *Richer, Wiser, Happier: How the World's Greatest Investors Win in Markets and Life* (New York: Simon & Schuster, 2021).

151 **"My father used to say":** "Mohnish Pabrai's Interview at Mint Equitymaster Investor Hour on April 11, 2023," *Chai with Pabrai* (blog), chaiwithpabrai.com/uploads/5/5/1/3/55139655 /mohnish_pabrais_interview_at_mint-equitymaster_investor _hour_on_april_11_2023.pdf.

151 **Pabrai graduated from high school:** Preston Pysh, "Mohnish Pabrai's Approach to Beating the Market," *Forbes,* January 16, 2017, forbes.com/sites/prestonpysh/2017/01/16/mohnish -pabrai/?sh=48e243dd3e01.

151 **In 1983, he entered:** "Mohnish Pabrai's Q&A Session with Students at Clemson University on January 27, 2021," *Chai with Pabrai* (blog), chaiwithpabrai.com/uploads/5/5/1/3/55139655 /mohnish_pabrais_qa_session_with_students_at_clemson _university_on_jan_27_2021_v2.pdf.

151 **His business offered IT consulting:** "Mohnish Pabrai, Managing Partner, Pabrai Investment Funds," Udemy, n.d., udemy.com/user/mohnishpabrai.

152 **Within six years, in 1996:** Inc. Staff, "The Inc. 500 Index," *Inc.,* October 15, 1996, inc.com/magazine/19961015/2077.html.

152 **One day, when he was waiting:** Nikhil Agarwal, "Man Who Made His Billions by Cloning Buffett, Says Shed Ego First to Get Rich," *Economic Times,* May 19, 2021, economictimes.india times.com/markets/stocks/news/man-who-made-his-billions

-by-cloning-warren-buffett-says-shed-ego-first-to-get-rich/arti
cleshow/82761893.cms.

152 **In 1999, he sold his company:** Vanya Gautam, "Mohnish
Pabrai: The 'Copycat Crorepati' Who Made Billions by Following Warren Buffett's Strategy," *India Times,* November 17, 2022,
indiatimes.com/worth/news/copycat-crorepati-mohnish
-pabrai-who-clones-warren-buffett-585048.html.

152 **He launched an investment fund:** William Green, "Turning $1 Million into $1 Billion by 'Cloning' Warren Buffett,"
LinkedIn, April 20, 2021, linkedin.com/pulse/turning-1-million
-billion-cloning-warren-buffett-william-green.

153 **"The good news is":** Green, *Richer, Wiser, Happier,* 35.

153 **Pabrai Funds achieved:** Agarwal, "Man Who Made His
Billions."

154 **Among these investments:** John Vincent, "Tracking Stocks
in Mohnish Pabrai's Investment Funds: Part III," *Seeking Alpha,*
October 10, 2011, seekingalpha.com/article/298573-tracking
-stocks-in-mohnish-pabrais-investment-funds-part-iii.

154 **"Once you undertake":** Chuck Chakrapani, *The Good Life
Handbook: Epictetus' Stoic Classic Enchiridion* (Toronto: Stoic Gym,
2016), 69.

156 **"I've seen dozens of silver bullets":** Howard Marks, *Mastering the Market Cycle: Getting the Odds on Your Side* (Boston: Houghton Mifflin Harcourt, 2018), 235.

156 **According to a *New York Times*:** Charles V. Bagli, "Nasdaq Adds the Biggest, Brightest Light to the Times Sq. Glare,"
New York Times, December 29, 1999, nytimes.com/1999/12/29
/nyregion/nasdaq-adds-the-biggest-brightest-light-to-the-times
-sq-glare.html.

157 **Instead, Seneca recommends:** Seneca, *Letters from a Stoic,*
trans. Robin Campbell (New York: Penguin Books, 2004), 64.

158 **As of July 2023, he had only:** "Mohnish Pabrai's Portfolio,"
ValueSider, accessed July 26, 2023, valuesider.com/guru/mohnish
-pabrai-dalal-street/portfolio.

159 **"All wish to possess knowledge":** "Thoughts on the Business of Life," *Forbes,* forbes.com/quotes/5755.

159 **"If you accomplish something good":** *Musonius Rufus: Lectures and Sayings*, trans. Cynthia King, (North Charleston, SC: CreateSpace, 2011), 91.

13. How to Start Investing in Stocks

165 **real estate historically has underperformed:** Over the long run, the S&P 500 has returned about 10 percent annually to investors on average versus just 3 percent or 4 percent for real estate. John Csiszar, "Should You Invest in Real Estate or the Stock Market?," *Yahoo! Finance,* January 24, 2023, finance.yahoo .com/news/invest-real-estate-stock-market-120027283.html.

165 **In 2023, you can contribute:** Adam Hayes, "401(k) Contribution Limits for 2022 vs. 2023," *Investopedia,* March 30, 2023, investopedia.com/retirement/401k-contribution-limits.

165 **Some employers match your contributions:** If your employer matches your 401(k) contribution, they will contribute up to a certain amount. This typically ranges from 4 percent to 6 percent of your salary. That means you can't save 20 percent and get another 20 percent from your employer. The percentage they match also differs per employer. With a partial match, your employer matches a percentage of your own contribution, often 50 cents for every dollar you contribute. A full match, also known as a dollar-for-dollar match, means your employer will match your contributions dollar for dollar.

167 **median household income of $80,893 a year:** Ironman at Political Calculations, "Median Household Income in February 2023," *Seeking Alpha,* April 4, 2023, seekingalpha.com/article /4592188-median-household-income-in-february-2023.

167 **The take-home pay:** The actual tax rate depends on the state where you live. This calculator uses an average tax burden of 29.14 percent. "Federal Income Tax Calculator—Estimator for 2022–2023 Taxes," Smart Asset, smartasset.com/taxes/income -taxes#if0RCFtLkp.

167 **Investing 10 percent a year, or $5,700:** Figures calculated with the investor.gov compounding calculator. "Compound

Interest Calculator," Investor.gov, investor.gov/financial-tools
-calculators/calculators/compound-interest-calculator.

168 **The average retired U.S. worker:** James Royal and Brian
Baker, "What Is the Average Social Security Check?" *Bankrate*,
July 13, 2023, bankrate.com/retirement/average-monthly-social
-security-check.

168 **For example, retired workers:** Social Security Administration, "Average Retired Worker's Monthly Benefit Is $1,164,"
Tampa Bay Times, April 28, 2010, tampabay.com/archive/2010
/04/28/average-retired-worker-s-monthly-benefit-is-1164.

168 **In 2023 retirees saw:** "CPI Inflation Calculator," U.S.
Bureau of Labor Statistics, bls.gov/data/inflation_calculator
.htm.

168 **In 2022, 66 percent:** Statista Research Department, "Homeownership Rate in the United States from 1990 to 2022," *Statista*,
February 6, 2023, statista.com/statistics/184902/homeowner
ship-rate-in-the-us-since-2003.

168 **In 2022, around 30 percent:** Katherine Hamilton, "Gen Z
Ahead of Millennials—and Their Parents—in Owning Their
Own Homes," *Forbes*, April 21, 2023, forbes.com/sites/kather
inehamilton/2023/04/21/gen-z-ahead-of-millennials-and
-their-parents-in-owning-their-own-homes/?sh=882c48a7d0e6.

14. Retire Like a Stoic

171 **U.S. Treasury bonds had an average:** "Historical Returns
on Stocks, Bonds and Bills: 1928–2022," New York University
Stern School of Business, January 2023, pages.stern.nyu.edu
/~adamodar/New_Home_Page/datafile/histretSP.html.

172 **The most used percentage:** Jasmin Suknanan, "What Is the
4% Rule and How Can It Help You Save for Retirement?"
CNBC Select, November 30, 2022, cnbc.com/select/what-is-the-4
-percent-retirement-savings-rule.

173 **"make ourselves flexible":** Lucius Annaeus Seneca, *On the
Shortness of Life: Life Is Long if You Know How to Use It*, trans. C. D. N.
Costa (London: Penguin Books, 2005), 90.

174 **"'When I am fifty I shall retire'"**: Seneca, *On the Shortness of Life*, 10.

174 **Most people are only ready:** Seneca, *On the Shortness of Life*, 11.

15. The 90/10 Rule of Speculation

176 **"If a thing is difficult"**: Marcus Aurelius, *Meditations*, trans. George Long (Standard Ebooks, public domain), 88, standard ebooks.org/ebooks/marcus-aurelius/meditations/george-long.

177 **bought shares of the gold-mining:** Theron Mohamed, "Warren Buffett Slashes JPMorgan and Wells Fargo Stakes, Bets on Barrick Gold," *Business Insider*, August 14, 2020, markets .businessinsider.com/news/stocks/warren-buffett-sells-jpmorgan -wells-fargo-buys-barrick-gold-2020-8-1029506182.

177 **sold the shares six months later:** Shubham Raj, "Does Warren Buffett's Short Honeymoon with Gold Signal You to Sell Yours?," *Economic Times*, February 19, 2021, economictimes .indiatimes.com/markets/stocks/news/does-warren-buffetts-short -honeymoon-with-gold-signal-you-to-sell-yours/articleshow /81105197.cms.

177 **The position represented a minuscule:** Berkshire Hathaway's total assets were $873.729 billion in 2020. "Berkshire Hathaway Total Assets 2010–2023 | BRK.B," MacroTrends, macrotrends.net/stocks/charts/BRK.B/berkshire-hathaway /total-assets. It purchased $562 million worth of Barrick Gold stock in 2020, so a $562 million position was 0.064 percent of Berkshire's total assets.

177 **the company's risk was minimal:** Maggie Fitzgerald, "Barrick Gold's Stock Soars More Than 10% after Buffett's Berkshire Reveals Stake," *CNBC*, updated August 19, 2020, cnbc.com /2020/08/17/barrick-golds-stock-soars-after-buffetts-berkshire -reveals-stake.html.

179 **"Money cannot consistently be made":** Jesse Livermore, *How to Trade in Stocks* (New York: Duell, Sloan and Pearce, 1940), 3.

179 **"Some speculators, known as 'panic birds'":** Edward Chancellor, *Devil Take the Hindmost: A History of Financial Speculation* (London: Penguin, 1999), 168.

179 **A common loss threshold:** The Investopedia Team, "Determining Where to Set Your Stop-Loss," *Investopedia,* June 4, 2023, investopedia.com/ask/answers/030915/how-do-i-determine-where-set-my-stop-loss.asp.

184 **"Concentrate every minute like a Roman":** Marcus Aurelius, *Meditations*, trans. Gregory Hays (New York: Modern Library, 2003), 18.

Conclusion: Be Like Granite

188 *If you own stocks:* Unfortunately, I can't find the source of this quote. I also don't know who the author was. I remember the writer was promoting gold as an investment instead of stocks. If you know the source, I would love to hear! Please get in touch through my website so I can update these notes.

Index

Italicized page numbers indicate material in tables or illustrations.